EXIT MINDSET

EXIT

~~OWNER~~

MINDSET

Unlock Profits,
Maximize Valuation, and
Live Life on Your Own Terms

REM OCULEE

LIONCREST
PUBLISHING

EXIT MINDSET

Unlock Profits, Maximize Valuation, and Live Life on Your Own Terms

FIRST EDITION

ISBN   978-1-5445-1990-6 *Hardcover*

         978-1-5445-1989-0 *Paperback*

         978-1-5445-1988-3 *Ebook*

I dedicate this book to the great instructors who have influenced my path: Sensei Nakayama Masatoshi, Sensei Nishiyama Hidetaka, and Sensei Teras Odisho. It is through their teachings of Shotokan Karate, accompanied with the timeless philosophies of martial arts, that I learned the true meaning of discipline, duty, and honor.

I also dedicate this book to you, the reader, and to all business owners who've worked tirelessly, surmounting hurdles and achieving victories.

I understand the magnitude of responsibilities you carry—for your family and your employees who rely on you. It transcends business; it's about the people you care for, their livelihoods, and security.

This dedication stands as an acknowledgment of your journey and the unsung heroes—your family and employees—who share it with you. This book, in essence, is a tribute to the intertwined lives and dreams that constitute the world of entrepreneurship.

CONTENTS

INTRODUCTION

IMAGINE HOW GREAT IT WOULD BE TO SEE EVEN more profits flow into your company. Imagine walking into the office and seeing that every unit of your operation is running smoothly. And imagine being able to step away from the company for a month or two without any negative consequences. Wouldn't that be amazing? How would you feel? How empowering and enriching would that be for you? This is the future you can create by developing an Exit Mindset. Not only can you create an incredible opportunity for your company now, but at the same time you can create exactly the situation potential buyers look for.

For better or worse, you may never know when you'll have to exit your business. Sometimes you choose your exit, and sometimes the exit chooses you. That's why it's important to cultivate an Exit Mindset long before an exit is even a consideration in your mind. Doing so is the surest way to guarantee that your business is worth the time and effort you have put into building it. This notion of worth may include personal pride or a sense of individual accomplishment, as well as the monetary gains through which you can effect positive change for your employees, community, and the world.

The Exit Mindset is the process of growing your business and then, if it's what you want, exiting with its deserved value in hand. It's an unconventional process. I created it to shake up the status quo approach of establishing a valuation for your business and then selling it. In my view, the two activities—growing your business and establishing a valuation for it when thinking about selling it—aren't separate concepts. You can use business valuation as a way to grow your company, whether you intend to sell it or not. By starting with the end in mind—combining a desire to win with a desire to accumulate wealth—you can expand your business horizons in ways you have never experienced, and enjoy the business you've created every step of the way. You accomplish all this by changing your perspective from that of a business owner to that of a business buyer. This change in perspective lies at the heart of the Exit Mindset.

This book represents over two decades of my own business and personal experiences. I have put an incredible amount of work into creating new companies, acquiring businesses, negotiating deals, and learning from my many successes and failures. Those experiences have led me to a better understanding of what does and does not work in business. I want to bring my unique experience to you to help you make your business better and achieve new levels of success.

When I started writing this book, I thought if I could help you improve on your results, then I would have done my work. But I came to realize there's much more to be gained. The lessons in this book can help you build a broader perspective, which can empower you to make decisions that have an impact not only on your business, but on your life.

The Exit Mindset is predicated on developing three core assets: an exit product, an exit infrastructure, and an exit conversation (which you have with your customers). Parts Two, Three, and Four of this book explain the principles behind those assets, and provide a detailed program and lots of advice on how to develop them. Together, the three exit assets—product, infrastructure, and conversation—form the backbone of your exit strategy.

But achieving all of that depends on you first developing an Exit Mindset. Without this mindset shift, without being able to objectively view, and value your business the way a potential buyer of it would, you are unlikely to achieve your ultimate exit goals. Part One of the book explains how to build this mental foundation. Once you've dropped the traditional owner's mindset for a buyer's mindset, you and your company are ready to develop your exit assets and are primed for explosive growth.

Finally, Part Five offers a wealth of hard-won advice on how to proceed once you're ready to sell your company. Now that the completion of your long-awaited goal of an efficient, scalable company is in sight, a great deal of thought and care needs to be put into your sales strategy—and all the while, you need to continue to effectively run your company in the same way that got you to this point. In Part Five I provide you with best practices for maximizing your company's valuation and negotiating with buyers. We'll also examine what you need to accomplish during each month of the sales process.

Now that you know the road map, it's time to get started. I'm certain that if you really take in, accept, and then implement the concepts presented in this book, the valuation of your company will grow. When it is time to cash out, there will be more "cash" to "out." And that alone is a worthy goal.

I endured thousands of hours of experience to develop some

of these strategies, but there's no reason you have to do the same. You can simply learn from what I've done. But remember, achieving isn't a spectator sport; it's an active, participatory sport. I can give you all the information, but you must pay attention, focus, and take action in order to develop an Exit Mindset. This book is only the beginning of your learning process. In addition to everything in these pages, check out ExitMindset.com for additional resources, and feel free to listen to the *Exit Mindset* podcast.

PART ONE

FOUNDATIONS OF THE EXIT MINDSET

CHAPTER 1

VALUING YOUR BUSINESS

LIKE MOST BUSINESS OWNERS, I NEVER THOUGHT too much about valuation. An earlier company I owned back then was moving along fairly well, and I was ready for an exit. I didn't anticipate any problems. I thought selling it would be simple. I'd just call a business broker, let them know I have a profitable business for sale, then get to work on my next venture while the broker facilitated the sale. What I didn't know is that there are many nuances that can make a sale problematic from a valuation perspective. I thought profitability was everything, but I later realized it is only one of many components (though an important one, for sure) considered in the valuation process.

What I realize now is that, while the company was doing well, I wasn't in the best frame of mind to sell my business. Psychologically, all I wanted to do was to move on. Once you embark on selling a business, it's hard to get yourself back into the mode of thinking required to continue running it. That's exactly what happened to me. As soon as I decided to sell, my mind and my concentration were focused on the next venture. Sure, I had to deal with certain things that were requested of me, but they weren't my top priority. In my mind, I was already out, and those responsibilities belonged to the next owner. This is why a business broker I know jokingly answers the question "When is the best time to sell my company?" by replying "The day after you start thinking about selling the company." Once you get into that mindset, all you can think of is the sale and what you are going to do after.

Busy with my next venture, I only periodically checked with my broker to see how things were going with the sale. There was some interest here and there, but nothing serious. The few offers I did receive weren't even in a range I could entertain. These potential buyers were "bottom fishers" who were simply looking to acquire companies significantly below their value. They have nothing to lose. If they get rejected nineteen times out of twenty, so be it. The twentieth time they get a company at a huge discount, so it's worth it!

Had I been in a different situation financially, I probably would have been very concerned by the slow movement on the sales front. I wasn't, but as time went by, the lack of interest did become an annoyance. Then it became a challenge. I started thinking, *Why isn't the company selling, and why isn't it selling for the price that I believe it should get?* It didn't make sense to me. After all, I had put a great deal of energy into getting my company to where it was. Wasn't that worth something?

Not necessarily. The hard truth was that my company wasn't valued by others for what I thought it was worth. I could imagine how valuable it was, I could dream about how much it was worth, and I could provide all the reasons and rationales as to why my business should be selling for the price I thought it should, but none of that makes a difference in the end. I'm not the only business owner to have thought this way, not by a long shot. That painful lesson taught me that there are universal truths about business valuation that wishful thinking cannot influence or change.

I began wondering what I was missing and what I could have done better to ensure the company was more attractive from a valuation perspective. How could I have made it worth what I believed it was worth without waiting until the very last minute to think about selling? How could I have built an exit-friendly company? To answer these questions, I began to research every aspect of what went wrong. I had to examine my decision-making process. In my mind, it was no longer about the money, but about discovery—I wanted to learn from my mistake.

I consulted with many people to find a solution to my dilemma. Each of them had a different way of looking at the subject, but none had a specific answer. So, I came up with a plan to take the best information I could get and create a model I could apply, not only to the current business I was exiting, but to any future businesses I might own. I sought out advice from other CEOs, business owners, brokers, investors, and private equity partners; I wanted to understand what they looked for in a business. What made them want to buy it? And what made them want to pay more?

I considered the most complex of strategies and the most basic. I used quantitative and subjective evaluations, meaning I sometimes conducted mathematical assessments and sometimes used analytical techniques that challenged conventional thinking. I learned a lot, but in the end, my research didn't yield a complete model for creating an exit strategy.

Then one day, as I was literally skiing down a slope, an

idea dawned on me: If thinking about an exit is so important throughout the life of a company, why not begin with an exit mindset from the start? Why not introduce and implement an exit mindset not on the day you decide to sell the company, but from the day you start or acquire the company? Had I done that, I realized, not only would I have been able to create a sound exit, but at the same time I would have shored up the foundation I needed to create a profitable business that allowed me the freedom and time to do more of the things I like to do. In that moment, everything I'd done for years came together. An Exit Mindset, as I thought of it, was now the tip of my spear and would become the driving force behind everything I would do.

It took years of further research, learning, and studying to understand how to make a company attractive to a buyer. One crucial discovery I made was that if you follow your instincts and employ sound strategies in building an exit-able business, you will generate even more profits, increase your company's valuation, and have more time for yourself and your family. In fact, you might enjoy your business so much that you don't want to sell it after all. That's the powerful flexibility of the Exit Mindset.

I did end up selling the business that started me thinking this way, but I didn't get the price I wanted. I learned from that. Since then, I've started, bought, and sold more companies. I have watched others do the same and have seen that they often repeat the same mistakes that had sabotaged my company's value. Most people had no idea what their companies were worth. If they did have an idea, it was usually the wrong idea; their companies routinely turned out to be worth much less than they thought.

UNDERSTANDING VALUATION

To understand and implement the Exit Mindset, you must first understand the concept of valuation. The valuation of your company is a core feature of the Exit Mindset, and a number you aspire to drive as high as possible. Valuation, to put it simply, is what your company is worth in the eye of a buyer. Your company's worth is not a set figure because different buyers can assign different values to it. But there are some common variables that determine what a company is worth to the buyer, including revenues, profits, the industry the company is in, intellectual properties, and assets. In many cases, a company's valuation is measured by objective data analyses. Some companies are sold by formula: two times revenues, or five times net profits, for example. If you apply the strategies in this book, you can increase that multiple.

SUBJECTIVE VS. OBJECTIVE VALUATION

While objective acquisitions understandably rely heavily on objective measures—the numbers—to justify the purchase, such measures are not the only factors in valuation. After all, any data model or set of numbers can be interpreted differently, making it virtually impossible to establish the "correct" price with any real certainty using only objective criteria. In many cases, valuation also involves a subjective analysis.

Reaching a reliable value, and price, depends heavily on the subjective analysis of people who assess the business beyond the numbers on the profit and loss (P&L) statement. While the search process for a new acquisition generally begins with buyers looking for companies that have favorable P&L statements or other metrics, that step is just an initial filter to help them zero in on potential acquisitions. Shortly after, the people involved in that acquisition, either formally or informally, apply the types of subjective analyses that I'll explain throughout this book.

Subjective analyses may weigh various tangible and intangible elements, such as how innovative the company's products are, the quality of its infrastructure, and the quality of the communication the company has with its customers or clients. All of these elements provide useful information to bolster the buyer's decision-making process. Often, these subjective components have a much greater bearing on the acquisition decision than the objective numbers alone.

The numbers are still important, but in the end, the numbers are the numbers. While you, as a business owner, will continue to pursue the growth of those numbers, intangibles such as potential scalability and the level of systemized infrastructure have the power to make a potential buyer take notice. When the intangibles are promising, buyers want to be part of the company's growth, and they will pay a premium for the opportunity.

BUILDING THE FOUNDATION OF AN EXIT MINDSET

The good news is that with this book in hand, you don't have to fall into the same time- and money-wasting trap I did. After sifting through thousands of concepts and hundreds of strategies during my research, I have distilled three essential themes to share with you: product, infrastructure, and what I define as the "conversation" a company has with its customers.

The products, infrastructures, and conversations described in this book are called **exit products**, **exit infrastructures**, and **exit conversations** because they focus on strategies that align with the three essential themes that define the Exit Mindset and will make a company attractive to prospective buyers.

If you deploy any one of these three strategies—an exit product, an exit infrastructure, or an exit conversation—you can certainly generate more profits, increase the value of your business, and create more personal time for other pursuits. Your business will be worth more when you sell. But if you can successfully deploy all three, you may create a business you love so much that you never want to leave it behind. I've seen it happen to business owners many times over the years—they suddenly recognize that their best asset is their business. Even if they sold it at a premium, they realized they would never get a better rate of return on their money from any other investment they might make.

Of course, there are other reasons to sell a company, and I am not suggesting that you have to keep it just because it is a good investment. But if you are able to follow the process laid out in this book, and if it provides you with a reasonably free personal life, you may want to look at this as more of a fun activity than another task to add to your grueling day-to-day work. By adopting and adhering to the Exit Mindset, you can create a company that is profitable and self-running. Does it get much better than that?

KNOW YOUR BUYER

The Exit Mindset principles apply no matter what kind of business you have, or what kind of buyer you're trying to sell to. They work for every type of acquisition, and for every size company. That doesn't mean you shouldn't tailor your approach according to your circumstances or the nature of the buying market. Keep in mind that different buyers have different motivations, but we can generally categorize them into three groups, as explained below. The sharper your understanding of the different types of buyers is, the better your prospects will be for selling your business at a premium.

The Flipper

One type of buyer walks into your company with the intent of buying your business solely to leverage a profitable exit as quickly as possible. They have a house flipper's mentality. They want to either beautify the business, chop it up, or fix it to make as much money as possible in the subsequent sale. Flippers are not typically interested in the personal side of the company or the company's purpose outside of making a return on their investment; they just want a number they can put on the balance sheet. They don't want to start companies; they want to own and profit from buying and selling them. The flipper mentality isn't good or bad; it is simply what it is. If you have been successful at adopting an Exit Mindset, your company will be perfect for this type of buyer because it will be scalable, systemized, most likely profitable, and won't require too much of their time and resources. You'll find these buyers are often represented by investment firms, angel investors, and private equity firms, among others.

The Integrator

Another type of buyer wants to integrate a similar or complementary business model into their existing infrastructure or product line. For example, a pharmaceutical company might purchase another pharmaceutical company and combine the two businesses. In this case, the exit product is the most important component to the buyer. However, if the business they're buying also has a top-notch infrastructure (an excellent product distribution network, for example) or a superior customer conversation (such as proprietary branding, name recognition, and market positioning) supporting the product, the buyer may decide to adopt it for their own business. Usually, a larger company acquires a smaller company, but you have probably seen examples of this type of transaction where smaller companies with financial resources gobble up a larger enterprise and morph into a new entity built on the acquired company's infrastructure. It's almost like a reverse acquisition. An integrator buys a company and becomes part of it.

The Participant

The third type of buyer, the participant, is one whose Exit Mindset is to personally grow and scale the business they plan to acquire. They care about the company and want to be a part of the day-to-day operations. That doesn't mean they want to step into unorganized chaos that could easily break down. No one buys a business so they can experience extreme difficulties. Participant buyers want the kind of business they also can exit someday.

CHOICES AND FLEXIBILITY

No matter which type of buyer you sell to, by following the Exit Mindset strategies, you can reach a higher company valuation. You can use these strategies to give yourself more peace of mind, knowing that when it's time to sell, you'll get a higher price for your company. And if you don't sell, you can still follow these strategies and enjoy all the benefits of generating even more profits *and* having a smoothly running company that offers you more time to spend as you like.

But isn't it counterproductive to focus on your exit while you're working hard every day to operate your business effectively? Most likely, an exit strategy isn't the first thing on your mind. It's a paradox, but the innovation of the Exit Mindset is that it's a change in focus that accounts for the plain fact that you won't be running your business forever. There will come a time when you may sell it or merge it with another company. Or perhaps you will decide to quit being a business owner to pursue other interests. You might also decide to sell your current business and go into another line of business, simply because you want a new challenge.

Planning for an exit might feel premature to you at the moment. Yes, you know it's going to happen someday, but that day probably seems so far in the future you don't even want to think about it right now. And that is where you could be making your biggest mistake. Because you shouldn't wait to develop an Exit Mindset. You should start thinking about it on day one. In fact, adopting an Exit Mindset early can establish the foundation needed to build a business that will run itself (a key feature that can greatly increase your business's valuation). A loss of operational focus isn't the risk you face right now. The real risk is that when you do exit, you will have undervalued your business instead of having continually created greater value by keeping the business focused under the guidance of an Exit Mindset.

Smart business owners start developing an Exit Mindset strategy from the moment their business idea is conceived. Their vision and mission statements use language like: "Once the company reaches a predetermined annual revenue of X, or annual profits of Y, we plan to put the company up for sale." This kind of thinking creates a dynamic that allows a company to grow from day one and avoid the lethargy created by the day-to-day grind.

Remember, gravity is a constant, and inertia is as much a rule of physics as it is a rule of human behavior. The status quo is seductive, and if you don't cultivate thinking that stimulates you and motivates you to the desired end, nothing great will happen. You must resist the temptation so many business owners fall into, thinking you can wait until "some other day." Instead, take immediate action and adopt a mindset that pushes you to accomplish what you've set out to do within a specific timeline, whether it's a revenue goal, a profit goal, or any other tangible, fixable milestone in the future. "Someday" doesn't count.

CHAPTER 2

DEVELOPING YOUR OWN EXIT MINDSET

SANDY WAS A HIGHLY SUCCESSFUL SPECIALIZED financial company owner. She worked in her business for over thirty years before deciding to sell. She told me that she had one big problem—the company was completely dependent on her, and no one else could carry the mantle. A buyer approached her; he was very interested in the company, but he quickly realized that it would be worthless once Sandy was gone. Sandy had no choice but to sell the company at a significant discount. Also, the buyer only agreed to the purchase if Sandy trained his team to replace her. In other words, the buyer already possessed an Exit Mindset strategy and wanted to structure a deal that would create an exit for himself, while Sandy got very little for her company.

After my conversations with her about the Exit Mindset, Sandy told me she wished we had talked two years earlier. She said things would have been a lot different for her, and her retirement could have been better. She was surprised at the relative simplicity of the concept, although she had never thought about it that way. She took what she learned from our conversations and helped point one of her friends, who has a business, to the Exit Mindset. Now her friend is building a stronger, more exit-able company.

Imagine taking a month off from your business. Would it survive? What about two months? Or six? Think about how your absence would affect operations, sales, and revenue. If you had to take an extended amount of time off, would you even have a business to come back to? If you truly believe you wouldn't, then now is the moment to start making changes so you never think that way again.

The Exit Mindset provides a dual function, creating two new dynamics for your business that will make it bulletproof when you are away. The first is establishing a high valuation early on, making your business attractive to buyers so you won't be scrambling when you think about exiting. If you follow the process correctly, the second dynamic is created by default: a self-running company. After all, that's what a potential buyer would like to see.

Think about it. There's a reason certain types of practices (like those of physicians, dentists, and attorneys) often don't sell for high revenue multiples in comparison to other industries: because most of them aren't self-running. They rely on one person or a few people. And should those key people leave, which often happens when a company gets acquired, the enterprise falters. The solution is to make your company a plug-and-play enterprise. A great way to demonstrate to a buyer that your company will continue to run, even if you or any of your key people leave, is to engage in a simple act of replacement. Probably one of the biggest tests of whether you have an exit-ready company from a valuation perspective is if you can take a six-month vacation and the company not only continues to operate but thrives and grows. Put another way, you should be able to just hand the keys to the new owner.

How involved do you need to be on a day-to-day basis to carry out the initiatives needed to scale your company, increase its valuation, and turn its infrastructure into a self-running proposition? It's a bit of a chicken-and-egg debate, isn't it? The operation needs you; therefore, you must work *in* it. But to achieve a self-running, scalable company capable of a high valuation, you must carve out time to work *on* it.

There is only one solution to this age-old dilemma. Decide on a course of action and implement it. Most of your successes come when you take the time to execute a plan. Stay focused and be motivated by all the additional benefits you get from developing an Exit Mindset: free time, improved quality of life, increased revenue, and the ability to engage in higher causes that you care about, whether in business or otherwise.

THE OWNER MINDSET

If you haven't yet adopted an Exit Mindset, then you're probably still in what I call an "owner mindset." While most people don't start a business with hopes and dreams of spending every day working in it, that is all too often what happens. Entrepreneurs know they'll have to put in the time to get it up and running, but they go in expecting to get to a point where they can step away. For many, that day never comes. They maintain the same pace—working *in* the business instead of *on* the business—for far too long, taking on more and more responsibilities. Their insider view of the business creates that owner mindset, and makes it impossible for them to think about the company from a buyer's point of view.

Daily tasks and "emergencies" act like a riptide that sweeps you into the ocean. You get caught in the flow of the day-to-day and are carried along. You are dragged away from your core mission of creating a valuable, self-running company. You fight and swim against the pull every day, but you make little progress, for one simple reason: fighting a riptide isn't the best way to break away from it. To escape an actual riptide, swim diagonally, away from the riptide channel, before heading to the shore. It's a simple strategy, but those who aren't aware of it usually drown. The Exit Mindset can function as this kind of rescue strategy.

As a business owner, you have a lot going on; you constantly solve problems and put out fires. It feels productive, but you will never solve them all or put them all out. Just when you think you got them all, another one appears. You can address day-to-day obligations and still make headway in the direction you want to go, but if you swim straight against the business riptide, you'll drown. Unfortunately, many business owners never manage to break out of this pattern. They never move beyond an owner mindset.

Business owners could break free by handing off most of the work to others, but sometimes they don't want to let go. Yet, if they looked around at their executive team, staff, and employees, they could identify people capable of carrying much of the workload. This would give them the boost they need to get out of the owner mindset, but making that move requires decision followed by action. Alas, comfortable chairs create comfortable people.

It's worth making the move to break free, however, because maintaining an owner mindset limits your options and inevitably leads to burnout. From a personal standpoint, it makes for an unhappy life. From a business standpoint, the owner mindset greatly limits your impact and leads to problems that never end. Putting out fires is a 24/7/365 responsibility. While you're doing that, your company's growth is limited. One person's time and energy can take a business only so far. If running the business requires your constant involvement, your ability to scale is greatly curtailed. You may believe you can do it all—and maybe you can—but now you need to redefine exactly what you mean by "all."

Settling into an owner mindset brings risk. Even if you like working endlessly every day and are happy with limited growth, you're still human. If you had a family emergency that took you away from the business, it could collapse. The value doesn't drop because everyone is upset about their leader's departure; it happens because there has been an overreliance on the leader (for both large and small tasks) and a failure to form the right teams to keep the business running. This can happen in organizations of all sizes. The owner mindset permeates any company when there's a lack of confidence in employees or an unwillingness to delegate. I've known businesses of around three hundred people that suffer a significant downturn when the CEO leaves.

Generally speaking, the bigger the company, the harder it is to break out of the daily grind and put some distance between yourself and the chaos. Business riptides in large companies come with high waves and a strong undertow that pulls leaders under. Even in large organizations, though, you can break free. You can't ignore the problems, but you can decide and take meaningful action to shift from an owner mindset to an Exit Mindset.

While good management is important, innovation is just as important. Businesses known for their great management aren't necessarily great businesses if they depend solely on that management to maintain their success. They must continue to innovate while great management steers that innovation. If you have an exit mindset, you will build a company that can continue to innovate after you sell it without relying on you alone to innovate.

THE BUYER MINDSET

There's another perspective we should pay attention to while developing an Exit Mindset: a buyer mindset. Thinking like a buyer encourages you to focus on the company's value from an outsider's point of view—someone who isn't emotionally attached to it, but is interested in how much profit it can generate and how much time, money, and effort that will require.

Before you take any practical steps toward running your business like a buyer, you have to shift your thinking. The journey toward a buyer perspective is continuous and has but one destination: achieving a scalable and profitable company with as high a valuation as possible. Such a company will have no shortage of buyer interest if you ever decide to sell.

A big part of this mindset shift involves escaping the day-to-day rat race described earlier. You begin to perceive how you can grow your business beyond the limitations of your own time. You don't have to be onsite every day. You don't have to be involved in every decision. The business doesn't come to a standstill when you take time off to focus on working *on* the company rather than in it. When you reach that point, your scalability improves—you can double or triple or multiply revenues by ten with the right combination of tactics. But you can't increase it tenfold if you are still in charge of everything. Remember, swimming against the riptide doesn't work. But smart execution at a level beyond that of an owner will change your life for the positive!

SHIFT YOUR MINDSET

To begin the journey to an Exit Mindset, start with your target in mind. Ask yourself some questions: *If I want to exit, at what price do I want to sell my company? Or do I want to keep the business but generate higher profits? Or do I want to take some time off, knowing that the company will be intact when I return?* You might eventually want to accomplish all three, and you can. Think about what's important to you.

Next, figure out what it will take to achieve these goals. Think strategically. These aren't tiny steps you'll be taking—you'll be looking at your business and your role through an entirely new lens. Owners often have a natural tendency to stick to their schedules, with occasional breaks to solve the problem of the day, but that gets you nowhere. Abandon that way of thinking. Look for the high-level changes that need to happen to move you massively forward, not in baby steps, but with giant leaps.

Hint: If you find yourself at your desk doing work that you do every day—you are still in the owner mindset. If your to-do list looks very familiar, you are still in the owner mindset. But if instead you are spending time working on problems you haven't worked on before—thinking about acquisitions, new products, new ways to market, and new markets to enter—then you are now in the Exit Mindset. Make sure you stay there at least half of every working day in the beginning, and then quickly make that grow to 75 percent of your time and then finally to 90 percent of your time.

The next step in planning your move to an Exit Mindset is to figure out exactly how to make that change happen. You know the why—now ask how. How do I make it happen? It's your business. You're in charge. You can do whatever you want, and the only thing standing in your way is you and your old owner mindset.

Where will you go? It can be tough to decide. Business can be like a jungle—sometimes you're surrounded by swamps, rivers, and alligators. Big alligators. You want to get out of there, but you don't know which way to go. Before you cross that river, wade through the swamp, or wrestle that alligator, take a higher-level perspective. Instead of running around, becoming more and more lost, find a tall tree and climb it. From your new perch, look around and survey the landscape. The jungle goes on for miles to the north, south, east, and—what's that to the west? A road? Yes, and there's a town at the end of it. Now you know which way to go. You have found yourself an exit strategy! Take a higher perspective on your strategy, and you'll find your path.

THE VALUE IN REEVALUATING

Nothing lasts forever. For example, let's say a company does everything perfectly. It's a flawless self-running company, boasts the right valuation, and everything is running smoothly. Does that mean the company has an infinite number of years to operate? If that were the reality, then perfectly built companies from the 1930s and 40s would still be here today. You and I know that isn't the case, except for a few outstanding exceptions.

What you need to achieve a self-running company with the right valuation is always changing. This is because of what I call "the ever-evolving business continuum"—the entire business landscape from consumer perceptions to new technologies to the world itself—where change is constant, and things are always shifting and moving in different directions. We must adapt to this multi-dimensional ecosystem in order to stay relevant in business. So pay close attention to what's around you. You may think you're making progress when you're actually stuck in one spot, and the deeper you dig in, the harder it is to get out. Instead of digging in deeper, you must be nimble; you must keep your valuation intervals (the time between the valuations) spaced in a way so you will be able to react, adapt more quickly, and avoid having to do an excessive amount of work.

Imagine you produced typewriters anytime from the early 1900s to the late 1970s. Your business did just fine because everyone was happy to have one, and they wanted more and more sophisticated features as time went on. Those businesses grew, until everything changed with the emergence of the personal computer in the early 1980s. At that point, users started to demand faster speeds, more pages, graphics, images—things typewriters simply couldn't do. One after another, major names fell: Facit, SCM, Olivetti, Remington. They did not adapt or pivot; they did not try to create a printer. Instead, Hewlett-Packard, Epson, Brother, and others started from scratch, building printers specifically for personal computers. The typewriter industry was wiped out within five years. These household companies that were once worth tens of millions sold for less than pennies on the dollar or completely went out of business.

Periodic re-evaluation of what potential buyers are looking for will help you keep the momentum you have already built. As your company grows, it will also evolve. Growth is natural when you are moving in the right direction. You will gain a new set of challenges that will disrupt the self-running aspect of the company. This means you will have to re-engage in the process. But when that happens, don't feel discouraged; the rewards will be there for you when you are ready to sell.

PART TWO

EXIT PRODUCT

CHAPTER 3

BUILDING YOUR EXIT PRODUCT

AS A BUSINESS OWNER, YOU DEAL WITH ALL parts of your company, some of them more than others. But one of the most important things to pay attention to and spend the right amount of time on is the product your company provides to the consumer—whether you're working in the B2B or B2C arena. Without product your company is nothing. **Product is king.** I could write a whole chapter with nothing but those three words repeated and still be understating the importance of an exit product. That's why it should be your top focus when considering your company's growth and your own exit strategy.

I call the kind of product you want to develop an **exit product**. An exit product refers to a product that your company produces that is desirable and sought after by buyers of your company because it has the potential to generate revenues and profits after your company is acquired by that buyer.

You may not have an exit product right now. If your product relies on your personal mental or physical labor on a daily basis, then it's not an exit product. If you are involved in the day-to-day selection, development, creation, and/or delivery of the product, it's not an exit product. If you want an exit product—the most important piece in the exit business puzzle—you have to take a hard look at what you have right now.

So how do you identify an exit product? You start with understanding a potential buyer's point of view. Do you have or can you develop (from scratch or by improvements) a product a buyer will want to keep on the market, improve, spin off into similar products, extend the geographical territories it's sold in, or expand the customer base to include other demographics?

It's important to identify what makes a product attractive to a buyer. What differentiates a "regular" product from an exit product? Chiefly, the way it connects with consumers. Consumers want product. They don't want your process. They don't want your employees, they don't want the marketing piece you send out, and they don't want your day-to-day problems. I'll even take it a step further—they actually don't want your product, per se. They want what your product *does*—they want something to ease their pain, solve their problems, or enhance their lives. If your product does any of these things, then you'll make the sale.

A product doesn't need to be a physical object. A service or an app is as much a product as any physical equivalent. For example, if an interior designer walked into your workplace and rearranged your furniture to make the space more pleasant and efficient, he or she provided a product—better interior design.

Whatever its form, an exit product (any product, for that matter) must be something people really want. Nothing will take a company to oblivion faster than marketing a product people don't want, one that sells only by the sheer force of marketing. Many companies that rely too much on marketing to sell products fall flat on their faces and never recover. Don't succumb to "shiny object marketing syndrome."

It's a myth that the right product sells itself. Few products sell themselves. Air and water could if someone had a monopoly on them because there's an immediate and uninterrupted biological demand for both, but, obviously, no one has a monopoly on them. Most products do not have that level of demand, and people have many choices. In a free economy, products and services are abundant. The only thing that encourages people to buy one instead of another is the additional value one product provides compared to its competitors. Some products enjoy a temporary advantage, when they're the only one of their kind available in the marketplace, but their dominance doesn't last. At some point, other companies notice the opportunity and release a competitive product to challenge it. These underdogs usually work hard at improving the features to gain market share, and that's when the competitive cycle starts.

If your company is caught in this cycle, be prepared to work hard without making a lot of progress. Over the years, I've seen many business owners struggle to sell their products, living in a constant state of stress and wondering why they have to go through so much to sell their products and why customers aren't flocking to buy them. Maybe the answer is that the business owner is looking at the whole concept of product from the wrong perspective.

Whether it's a physical object or an app or a service, an exit product must be something valued by both consumers and potential buyers of your business. It must be something they really want, something that they perceive as delivering additional value. Be assured, buyers will notice if your product is not doing a good job connecting with consumers. Remember, an exit product is appealing to buyers of your company because they recognize its intrinsic value stemming from its strong connection to customers and its potential for further growth.

YOUR EXIT PRODUCT MUST PROVIDE LIFE-CHANGING SOLUTIONS

To be successful with your exit product, you need to get into your consumer's mind and understand their need to see value in what they purchase. People want life-changing solutions. If they can't get a life-changing solution, they at least want to remove their pain, and they want that relief now. By "life-changing," I don't necessarily mean something earthshakingly important; even products that provide solutions to small daily problems play an important role in the marketplace. The most common mistake business owners make is providing products that don't make the consumers' lives better.

Any product could provide life-transformational value in some way, but customer *perception* is what really determines their value: Even if you think you are providing a high level of value to a consumer's life, they may not agree. Your consumer is probably not crunching mathematical equations to decide if your product is good for them and their circumstances. Their response boils down to a perception, a thought, a feeling based on their experiences and attitudes.

A good example of how consumer perception works is the difference between Corvettes and Mustangs. Both are similar performance automobiles, but some people prefer the sleek Corvette and others the muscular Mustang. These preferences are often quite strong. But the point is that, regardless of their preferences, consumers perceive these cars as providing life-transforming value. And it is up to the company to understand this and produce products that fulfill such consumer needs and aspirations.

It's not what you think that matters, it's what *they* think. How well you understand what makes a transformational difference for them is what determines whether they will buy from you. Transformational value can come in many forms, and is provided whenever a product or service creates enough of a difference in the customer's life. The change may be small or large. It may be a better razor or a bigger home. In both cases, a life is transformed in some way.

People want solutions that make their lives better, easier, and more fulfilling. If you understand that, you can rework your entire product focus toward creating a feeling of personal advancement and satisfaction—transformation. That's the way toward making an exit product. But how do you do that?

THINK BACKWARD!

Essentially, you start at the end of the product development process and build backward, reverse-engineering your product. This isn't the conventional strategy, but I've seen the conventional strategy fail countless times. And here's the kicker: Engaging in back-to-front development works for any product, including your business. Approach your business as a transformational product. Imagine the changes it brings about and build it from that point back to its origin. In this case, the Exit Mindset will help you achieve higher revenues, more success, and a desirable product line, ensuring you are prepared if someone approaches you to buy your company.

STAND OUT FROM THE CROWD

Here's another key consideration for developing your exit product: When consumers don't buy your product, it's because they don't perceive it as the solution they need, or because they see someone else's product as a better one. This is true in your own experience, isn't it? Many companies can sell you a cell phone, but I bet you can think of one, in particular, that represents the best of the best for your situation. Maybe it's transformational because of the quality, the price, the features, or any one of a number of things. In the end, you buy it because the product, in your own mind, will give you life-transformational value in the form of making your day easier. You may not be consciously aware of your motivation at the moment of every purchase, but I can assure you it is your innate thought process, whether you're considering Tesla vs. Volt, Apple vs. Android, or G-Suite vs. Office Suite. You weigh your decision according to what best fits your needs and wants. To create a transformational product—an exit product—in a world full of similar products and competitive forces, you must create a way to help the consumer separate you from your competitors.

Look for ways to take an ordinary product and make it stand out in the marketplace. Imagine that it's desirable to a specific demographic, or multiple demographics, who will generate the revenues you look for. If you were in the wine business, for example, what could you do to distinguish your product from all other sellers out there? You might decide to make your product a personal experience instead of just a commodity by offering ancillary services around the sale. Perhaps you could carve a niche by offering only the best choices, customized for each specific customer.

It comes down to this: Evaluate your product. Is it what the customer truly desires? On a scale of one to ten, desire for the product must be at least an eight to qualify as an exit product. If your product has achieved that level of desire with the right consumer avatar, then determine whether you have distinguished it enough to establish sufficient consumer demand to ensure its position in the marketplace.

TO BUY OR NOT TO BUY

Ultimately, enough people have to desire your exit product to generate enough sales without your company having to employ an extensive salesforce. The sales channel should highlight what the product does for the customer and how well the product does it. The customer shouldn't have to be over-sold to realize the benefits.

To determine if your product has achieved your stated value proposition and the market distinction you seek, ask yourself, *Is my sales team struggling to convince customers to buy the product?* Great products may not sell themselves, but they practically sell themselves if you show their features to the right consumer.

Some signs that might tell you that you're on the right track are the "buying questions" customers regularly ask. Examples include: Does it come in different colors? Does it have technical support? How long does delivery take? These questions provide valuable information about your buyers; nobody would ask them unless they were interested in buying. If your product has immediate appeal among the appropriate consumers, you'll hear a lot of these sorts of questions. If your product has no distinctive elements, in the mind of the consumer, those buying questions won't come up simply because the product doesn't interest them in the first place. Your objective is to refine your exit product so that when a customer comes across it, it automatically triggers those buying questions.

To reiterate a point made earlier, there are two key reasons consumers make a purchase. Ideally, your business would combine both and provide a highly desirable product for the right demographic segment you are targeting. The first reason consumers make a purchase is that the product fulfills that person's needs (regardless of whether or not the product is the best in its class). For example: If Product A is the best in its class and something your customer needs, but it's designed for a different age group, they may choose Product B, even if it is of lesser quality, because it provides transformational value for their age group.

The second reason people make a purchase is if the product taps into an innate desire to solve some issue in their lives that the customer wants to see changed or improved. It's not so much about how the product functions. A product might function very well and deliver something that helps the customer achieve a result. But often, that result doesn't address what the consumer *perceives* as a pressing need, so they can do without it.

What you want to do is tap into a desire and ensure your product fulfills that desire. You also have to consider whether the customer is willing to spend part of their hard-earned money to acquire what your product offers. Since you can't increase the customer's financial resources, you only have one way to persuade them to purchase your product—maximize the amount of perceived life-transformational value you give them so they have reason enough to purchase your product.

What's going on in the customer's mind when they're making this decision to buy or not to buy? They are making a binary conclusion about every product that comes to their attention—often subconsciously. The answers to their basic yes or no questions are crucial—they will determine whether they consider the purchase or not, and they happen within a millisecond. Those questions include the following:

- Is this worth it?
- Does it help me?
- Is this going to change something in my life?
- Is it worth spending the money on?

If the answer to any of those questions is no, then the customer won't purchase your product. Your mission, as a business owner creating an exit product, is to turn those answers into a yes for the right consumer—for millions of right consumers.

Your objective is to establish market dominance with your exit product. Keep in mind, market dominance is less about the volume of units you sell and more about combining volume and pricing to reach an optimal profitability point. Give the product as many features as you can, as long as they're relevant to your target demographics at the best price possible, relative to quality. Be careful, though. When I talk about the best price, I don't necessarily mean the lowest price. I mean the best price relative to what your market can absorb and to the value of what your product can deliver.

You can land on the correct features and best price by considering the reasons people buy products. Typically, people buy either for utility (usage value) or vanity. Sometimes it's both. For example, a person buying a chainsaw is probably buying for utility. A person buying a coat may be doing the same—they don't care if the coat looks good or not; it's meant to keep them warm. On the other hand, sometimes they buy the coat because it looks great on them—they're buying for vanity. Maybe the coat looks good and keeps them warm—what a deal!

Balance utility and vanity to get the best result. It's your mission to determine the proportion of those two elements in your product and modify that balance to maximize the value your consumer desires and convince them to choose you over your competitor.

A potential buyer of your company will certainly take time to understand your company (your product) and the market it operates in. They will also keenly analyze your exit product and its appeal to consumers. In implementing an Exit Mindset strategy, you determine the value of your company by what you do. The buyer should not have to invest more than a short amount of time to understand the product or the market.

THE IMPORTANCE OF A FAN BASE

The prospective buyer of your business will want to know that your company has value well into the future. That means having repeat customers for your exit product. Your buyer will know that repeat business and lifetime consumers are significantly more cost effective and more profitable for a company, and that without repeat customers they will have to worry about continually finding new customers. That's why many companies today adhere to a model that will generate ongoing revenues from existing customers—from their "fans." To do that, these companies must provide a valuable product that appeals to the customer and keeps them interested in continuing to purchase it. If the company mismanages its relationship with consumers, consumers will buy from a competitor or quit buying altogether.

In today's competitive environment, it's even more advantageous to build repeat customers than to continuously sell to new people. Many companies have recognized this truth and have created a subscription model for products that they previously sold individually. But the subscription model is not the only option. If the subscription model is not viable for your situation, you can still build repeat business. I'm sure you've repurchased a product several times simply because you became a fan of the value it provided. Notice I didn't say you were a fan of the product; you're really a fan of the solution (although you could be a fan of both). The product provides a solution to you that you find valuable, and as newer editions continue to deliver that value, you will likely continue to purchase it. Just think about all the people who upgrade their phones every time a new version arrives.

The Exit Mindset relies on the same principle: creating solutions that create loyal fans. Provide consumers with a product whose features and benefits create transformational value above what other products give them. The moment you accomplish that, hold on to it and keep improving as best you can. Remember, your competitors are right behind you, and they're watching your business grow. If you're in a competitive industry and you have the edge, competitors will do everything they can to bring their products to a value level equal to or higher than your own. They might develop more features, lower pricing, or hit you hard by offering both! When that happens, your business must rely on customer loyalty.

You can see all of this in the actions of Apple Inc. At this stage of the company life cycle, Apple has a huge fan factor—a person who buys one of their products will very likely make a repeat purchase, and perhaps buy other types of products from them. And Apple maintains an entire product ecosystem—it designs its products to work together—to strengthen its relationship with its fans.

You can be sure that any potential buyer of your company will be interested in your data about how your fan base responds to product releases and improvements. This will obviously increase what you can ask for the company. As you analyze your product's fan base, ask yourself, *Would a buyer find these results convincing, profitable, and sustainable?* If you see room to improve, then make those considerations part of your strategy for moving toward an exit product.

CHAPTER 3 *EXERCISE*

Take Action :

Exercise Questions: Analyzing customer behavior and enhancing product appeal for potential buyers

What are the reasons people buy your product? If unclear, how can you better understand their motivations?

What are the reasons people do not buy your product? If there are barriers, how can they be mitigated?

Why might customers prefer competitors? If there are advantages, how can you match or exceed them?

What are three strategies you could employ to increase your product's attractiveness to potential buyers?

How can you increase motivation for purchases? If methods are lacking, what new strategies could be deployed?

THINK PRODUCT REVENUES

SO FAR, IN OUR JOURNEY TO THE EXIT MINDSET, we've talked about "value" and "product." In this chapter, we'll reconsider the conventional understanding of another term: revenues. We most often refer to revenues as "sales revenues," but that phrase doesn't focus on the tip of the spear, which is actually "product revenues."

What do I mean? First, let's ask, "What are sales?" Sales simply refers to the movement of the product between two parties. Your product is the source of your company's earnings. As I said previously, product is king, and the better your product, the more revenues you will be able to generate. Of course, there are other things that go into the mix, such as services (which are products in themselves). But great companies aren't built on mediocre products. They are built on products that offer customers the best choice (or the only solution) in the industry in which they compete. The impact of your product affects more than your revenues and your current profit-and-loss statement. Your product is what makes your company attractive to a potential buyer.

Much of the work you do to develop an Exit Mindset is to shift your thinking so that you're looking at your company and business from an owner's point of view to a buyer's point of view. In the sixth century, Sun Tzu, one of the greatest warriors of all time, wrote in his book, *The Art of War,* "You should always gain the higher ground in order to win the battle." That's precisely what you're working for in adopting an Exit Mindset. You want to be on higher ground. You want to take a bigger perspective on your company—occupy a superior vantage point and exert more control over all aspects of selling your business.

For instance, maybe the revenues among your company's products vary a lot. This is quite common for businesses selling multiple products. One obvious possibility for this variance could be that one of your products doesn't sell as many units. That's not necessarily bad. Take the time to carefully analyze that product's *full* impact on your business. Perhaps you'll conclude that, yes, maybe only a small segment of your customer base is interested in that particular product, but your analysis shows that this customer segment also tends to go on to purchase other products your company sells. So the result of your viewing things from "higher ground" is that you can now point out to a potential buyer that even one of your low-revenue products is an asset, since it leads to generating higher revenues through customers purchasing additional products your company sells. You can also point out that a by-product of all this is a decrease in the cost of acquiring customers for those additional products.

Another aspect of having a bigger perspective is objectively understanding the goals and concerns a potential buyer might have about your business. Every business has weak spots. If you recognize possible objections buyers might bring up, you can resolve them ahead of time. For example, customer acquisition is one of the most important elements under consideration by a potential buyer, and no purchaser wants a company that has consistent difficulty acquiring new customers, has high customer acquisition costs, or has high customer turnover. So you must keep in mind that the product itself is part of your customer acquisition strategy. Regardless of precisely what the customer purchases, you have built an ongoing relationship that could turn into future product sales, as long as you handle the relationship correctly. The more easily and efficiently your business model acquires a new customer, the more valuation accrues to your company. Here's an Exit Mindset bonus: this works even if you don't want to sell your company—if you have a good customer acquisition strategy, your company is more profitable.

Consider this contemporary example: Before Siri was an Apple product, it was an inexpensive app available for download. Apple did a great job in recognizing that even though the app wasn't immediately popular, it had a unique product value. It just needed to be improved, packaged, and promoted in the right way. Apple, with its broader perspective, saw Siri's potential and bought it. The value Apple derived from Siri was significantly more than the price it paid. So even though Siri wasn't making a lot of profits for its original creators, Apple knew it could leverage the product and extract much more revenue from it.

Potential buyers of your company want to know whether it's bringing in acceptable levels of revenue and whether it will continue to bring in revenue. If you're developing an exit plan for your business, ask yourself, *If I wanted to sell my business today, would my product be viewed favorably? Does it have a future in the marketplace? What's its growth potential?*

WHO IS THE RIGHT CUSTOMER FOR YOUR EXIT PRODUCT?

Potential buyers will look hard at the customers who purchase your product. The questions a potential buyer may ask include: *What does that customer segment look like? Is it shrinking or growing? Is it a demographic that will continue to buy the product or age out of it? Is there another potential market for this product?* And most importantly, *who are the current or potential competitors for this product and have any gained a foothold in the marketplace and among this demographic?*

A buyer evaluates your customer segment both objectively and subjectively. From an objective standpoint, they'll look at the data on your product and similar products. *What's the customer demand like? Is it increasing or decreasing?* If the product is new to the market and there is little data, they rely on their subjective perspective. A potential buyer will also ask, *What do I believe is the life of this product and how do I think it will perform during its lifetime?*

From an Exit Mindset perspective, you might ask yourself, *Do I have the optimal product for the right consumer?* The best exit product must be a product that a potential buyer of your company finds appealing from a valuation perspective. But you can only create that if your product features and benefits match the demographics and psychographics of your consumer. Your product must have strong consumer appeal, meaning it has earned the highest approval in its category and is priced correctly for the consumer marketplace.

Pricing is an area that requires particular thought and care.

Often, a company owner puts a new product (an improved version, for example) on the market and prices it a bit higher than the previous version. The product sells well until competitors emerge. The owner assumes his customers will remain loyal, but often this approach backfires. Unless the product or the company has a special benefit to the consumer, the business will ultimately lose customers from incorrect pricing.

You have to adopt both a scientific and intuitive approach toward product creation, evaluation, and deployment. To arrive at the optimal exit product for the right consumer, start by breaking down the basic elements of your product's features and benefits. Next, evaluate each element by relating it to the target demographics, focusing on current customers first and then on potential customers. You also need to consider some of your consumer psychographic data in your exit product design. For example, investigate what kinds of magazines your customers subscribe to, what kinds of health and fitness levels they desire, and other lifestyle markers. There's a large amount of psychographic data you can pull from to gain a sophisticated understanding of what your consumer is interested in so you can design your product specifically for them. Additionally, examine every feature and benefit your product offers and run them against a demographic characteristics filter, something I call "demographic relatability."

This advice may sound obvious to you, but I can't tell you how many times I've seen business owners build a product that's not optimally configured for the right people, or is optimally configured but for the wrong people. Only by being candid with yourself and making the right assessments will you arrive at the right product design and sales profile.

HOW YOUR EXIT PRODUCT AFFECTS YOUR COMPANY'S BOTTOM LINE

To make the right decisions during the exit process, you must always be aware that any potential buyer of your company will analyze how your product affects the company's bottom line. Buyers might ask to sit in with the sales department to see what is selling or to stand behind the register to watch what people are buying. They might even want to sit with a receptionist to see what goes on in your company during the day. Earlier I mentioned that buyers evaluate your company both objectively and subjectively. These are the kinds of subjective things smart company buyers do to supplement the numbers the company owner gives them.

Because a buyer considers your business from many angles, you must also look at your bottom line from a variety of perspectives. For instance, let's step away from the customer acquisition perspective we took above and examine your bottom line from the perspective of how pricing and revenue generation interact. You might have multiple products, all of them losing money except for one that is generating the bulk of your revenues. That doesn't sound great. Or does it? Believe it or not, that situation could be acceptable if one of the products that is losing money acts as a lead-in to your winning product in proportions that create a surplus of revenues for you.

Consider how fast-food chains operate, for example. Many of them are not making—or in fact are losing—money on selling their signature item. If that were the only product they were selling, they would not be able to operate at the levels they do. However, high profit margins from the sale of sodas, fries, and additional snacks allow them to be profitable. In other words, the main product is a lead-in to the more profitable add-on products. If you take that model and apply it to your business, you could create success beyond your expectations.

There are other instances where unprofitable, break-even, or slightly profitable product sales lead to an upsell toward the main profit-driving product. Why, for instance, are casinos happy to give you a hotel room at a steeply discounted price compared to non-casino hotels of a similar caliber? Because rooms aren't their main profit driver. It's not even what they want you to buy. They simply use discounted rooms to attract you to the gaming tables. That's where they make the bulk of their profits.

There are many other pricing models that you can deploy. What's important is how your buyer sees it playing out. Buyers might focus on your main product to see how they can make it even more profitable. Or they might look at whether it's worth keeping the other products. They might try to discern whether the company would be more valuable if it put its resources behind the highest revenue product. Or, the buyer might see opportunities for massive profitability if they took the product to other sales channels and integrated it with them.

Even if you consider all aspects of exit product decisions, the outcome is never guaranteed. That's just how business is! For every business decision you make, you're a hero if it works and a zero if it doesn't. In business, you succeed by the ability to make decisions that others can't—or won't. Sometimes you have to step away from a situation and seek a different perspective to see what kind of problems affect the attractiveness of your product to buyers. Start analyzing your product line and determine your main revenue generator. If you have secondary products that are significant from a revenue perspective, then add them to this thinking process.

It's possible that your analysis may uncover that your company is experiencing certain hidden losses. In my *Exit Mindset* podcast, I talk about "phantom losses." These are losses that you don't see because the business never materialized in the first place. You're not aware of these losses, but let me assure you, they *are* losses and they have consequences. You might as well have burned the money.

It can be challenging to identify phantom losses. Sometimes they occur in areas where you actually could identify them, but you are so close to those areas that you may not have the right perspective to see them. For example, a few unnoticed simple tweaks to your production flow could double or triple your revenue. These are losses in the sense that you are missing out on all the potential gains you could have had if you had paid closer attention. Alternatively, sometimes phantom losses occur because you are not staying focused on your core product mission. You're getting sidetracked by things that don't deliver real growth to your company, and are losing out because that time and investment could have been applied to evolving and improving your key products.

You might find that you need some mental distance to develop a detached view of your company's situation. Carve out some quiet time for yourself. Reflect on the products and services you offer and the revenues they generate. Consider potential phantom losses. It is only by holding an honest image of your business and its daily operations in your mind that you can cultivate the Exit Mindset that will make your business a standout to future purchasers, all while maximizing profits you can enjoy in the meantime.

CHAPTER 4 *EXERCISE*

To align your view of your customers and products with a potential buyer's perspective, ponder these questions:

Would a potential buyer agree that your company's demographics align with your business goals? If not, what actions will you take to rectify this perception?

Do you think potential buyers would feel confident in scaling the company based on your current consumer demographic data? If not, what actions will you take to improve your demographic data?

Can you precisely identify your customers and the strategies to reach similar demographics without over-reliance on advertising or sales staff? If not, what actions will you take to enhance your customer identification and recruitment strategies?

What is the specific problem your product solves for its intended customer?

How does your product alleviate your customers' pain points? If it does not, what actions will you take to address this?

In what ways does your product enhance your customers' quality of life? If it does not, what actions will you take to improve this?

How does your product offer transformative value to your customers? If it does not currently, what actions will you take to enhance its transformative value?

CHAPTER 5

EXIT PRODUCT STRATEGIES

AT ITS CORE, AN EXIT PRODUCT STRATEGY RELIES on your ability to gather data, analyze your situation, take a buyer's mindset, and implement a plan. We've discussed what makes a business attractive to buyers—a solid revenue stream that isn't reliant on the owner or a single product; a keen understanding of customers and why they are buying your products; and a management infrastructure that isn't dependent on your presence to keep things going.

Many factors affect how your buyer perceives the value of your company, but few companies have been bought simply because they had built a strong infrastructure or facilitated a great conversation with the consumer. After all, absent a great product, a conversation about something worthless is worthless itself. The conversation must start with product.

YOUR PRODUCT'S INTANGIBLE VALUE

By developing a product that helps the consumer and creates demand, you fulfill the ultimate noble aspect of business—helping people solve a problem or otherwise get something they need or value in their lives. Very often, the subjective value your customer receives from your product is much greater than the money they spent to buy it. Maybe your product can improve someone's emotional well-being, for example—that's the real value. If you've created a zip line attraction, you're not renting ropes and pulleys. You're not even selling an incredible ride. What you are selling is a positive experience—your customer comes to you for the thrill, the satisfaction, or maybe just the plain old happiness that riding your zip line brings them. There's no tangible product. People don't go home with their very own zip line. But what can be more valuable than a fun experience and all of its memories?

Don't underestimate the significance of your intangibles. For instance, your own expertise can be uniquely valuable. Be aware of this, and don't undercut yourself and the intangible value that only you can bring to people's lives. I can't tell you how many times I've watched people shortchange the worth of what they deliver because they don't fully grasp the value of their services, and they don't feel they deserve a lot from the customer. They subconsciously suffer from "low business self-esteem." They don't believe their expertise is worth market value. If that's your way of thinking—what I call the "martyr" mindset—you're setting yourself up to earn less than fair value. When you don't earn what your services are worth, you shortchange your own growth, your employees, and all the people counting on you.

Years ago I heard a story about a TV repairman that illustrates this idea. This repairman was asked to fix a broken TV (of course). Within minutes of entering the customer's house, he had opened the TV, changed a small wire, closed the TV, and turned it on. It was back in perfect working order. The repairman then handed a bill for $100 to the customer, at which point the customer gasped, "You only changed a small wire worth five cents and you are charging me $100?" The repairman calmly and politely replied that he didn't charge $100 for the wire. He only charged five cents for that. But he indeed charged them $99.95 for knowing which wire needed replacing.

The point of this story is to show you how an intangible (in this case, expertise) justified the price of the repairman's product. He knew which problem to solve and how to solve it, even if the actual fix was simple. That knowledge had to be worth something; after all, if it were so easy, the TV owner could have solved it himself. It's true that you can solve any problem, given enough time and resources, but it might take hours, days, months, or years trying to figure it out. You can spend that time and avoid paying a repairman $100. But this logic also works in reverse. What opportunities were forever lost to you because you devoted hours to researching this one problem?

You must value your services reasonably and well. You should not overvalue them, and you should not undervalue them. And you should understand why others charge what they do for their services.

KNOW YOUR PRODUCT

Evaluating the likely success of your own product is crucial to your decision-making as you build out your exit product strategy. To increase the chance that your decision will produce the best outcome, you need a deep understanding of how the product evaluation process works.

When we evaluate something, we are guided by our belief systems regarding what is good and bad, right and wrong. That sounds objective, but often it's unintentionally subjective because the judgment is colored by perceptions and beliefs that we might not even be aware of.

As a business owner, your job is to use common-world objective measures and rationales to sift through potential ideas and assessments to reach what I call the "reasonable standard." That means you have to behave as though you are an outside observer, even though you, as the one most affected by this decision, are definitely on the "inside." To make good decisions, you must cultivate a dual mindset in your thinking: one side is always analyzing, while the other is judging the analysis to see if it reasonably solves the problem.

One side of your decision-making insists on meeting a reasonable standard, but must make adjustments to the analytical side of your process. This may seem like a convoluted explanation, but it's really common sense (even if you've never thought of it this way before). We are always in dialogue with ourselves, posing questions and pondering answers. In fact, everything you do happens as the result of a series of questions and answers. How do I solve the problem in front of me? Do I go left, or do I go right? Did I make the correct decision? Your brain is constantly engaged in answering these sorts of questions whenever there is a decision to be made. You might not realize that this process is happening, but trust me, this is all going on continuously at a subconscious level.

In the case of your business, one critical decision you face is deciding if you are developing the right product. The question you must ask is, Does my product meet the criteria I need to achieve market dominance? Answer honestly. Answer objectively. But answer subjectively, too. Use whatever data you have available, but recognize that you can't run a business only by numbers (if you could, CPAs would run the world). You know instinctively whether your product really is distinct from others in the marketplace.

Let's say, for example, that you're in the business of selling vitamins. Your initial development might focus on the fact that everyone needs the vital nutrients that vitamins contain. You realize your market share can be huge. You're tempted to focus on the importance of the product to this gigantic market, but what you should focus on is answering these two questions: How realistic are my chances of becoming a dominant force in the vitamin supplement industry? How can I design my product to differentiate it from other vitamin products so that consumers see it as a solution to a particular problem they have?

Once you have the answers, you're closer to product clarity. You're on the road to recovering from a non-exit product that won't do your valuation any good and moving toward an exit product that gets you a better price if you sell your business or better product revenues if you don't.

CONTINUOUS DEVELOPMENT

Evaluation and development don't end when you bring a successful product to market. As previously discussed, there are always competitors who will come behind you and focus their product development on ways to make their product different from and an improvement on your own. Steve Jobs was famous for putting the idea of planned obsolescence into practice at Apple. Apple is always designing the next iteration or the next product line. The philosophy of continuous improvement is captured in the Japanese concept of *kaizen*, which is the philosophy of continuous improvement: Accept that your product is not going to be perfect forever; it is only perfect for today. Adopting this point of view will keep you on your toes, ready to sprint forward, while your competitors sit on the sidelines, satisfied and relaxed—or mystified as to what you'll do next.

To maintain *kaizen*, make the research and development (R&D) portion of your operation an active component of your business. Don't think of development as a pipe in which research and development are at one end and sales and marketing at the other. Encourage all of these stakeholders to be continually working together, thinking and sharing new product ideas and improvements. The investment to do this doesn't have to be huge—you might not require a large R&D group. You might get all the answers you need by allocating a certain amount of time to think about the issues and needs your consumers bring to your attention, either through direct interaction with them or from market research. These answers should inspire ideas for improving your product.

Even a relatively simple improvement, such as combining a number of elements in your product, can speak to your customers in an entirely different way. And in that difference there is value.

To maintain clarity as you move forward, create a product road map that describes precisely what your product will look like. This document will provide a guiding vision, a "north star" that you can follow to your ideal exit product and exit strategy. Your road map also helps you communicate with potential company buyers when you need to demonstrate the opportunities that lie ahead for them.

Key questions for optimizing your product and engaging customers:

Is there any aspect of your product that is hard to use or apply? If yes, what modifications will you make?

Which product benefits are vital and why?

What consumer problem should your product eliminate?

Which benefit most interests the consumer?

What should your product help the customer achieve, save, or gain?

Does your product need simplification or changes? If yes, what changes will you implement?

What elements of your product should be removed or added? If applicable, what is your plan for this?

What is the main complaint about your product? How will you address it?

Why are some potential users not utilizing your product? If there is a reason, what is your strategy to involve them?

Are there inconsistencies in your product? If yes, what steps will you take to address them?

HOW TO MAKE HIGHLY PROFITABLE PRODUCTS

THE ULTIMATE PURPOSE OF A BUSINESS IS TO generate a profit while providing great products for the consumer, taking care of employees, and helping the community in which the business operates. Profit is key to all this. As you build out your exit product strategy, profits generated from your products are key to understanding the full value of your business. But to have profitable products, you first need to carefully evaluate your current products to assess what their potential is.

As this chapter will detail, the initial product evaluation process involves analyzing a number of factors. You will examine product sales data, consumer demographics, and industry data. You will review internal team assessments. You can look at any pertinent product data you have at your disposal. Together, these methods of analysis will tell you a lot about your product.

During this phase, you will turn to the consumers who are using your product and begin testing. For example, you might create multiple variations of the product you are currently selling or developing and test those versions on different customer groups. Put those findings together with some industry data to better understand which versions your customers prefer, which they don't, and why. Later in this chapter, we will explore ways to evaluate your product and adapt it based on those findings.

EVALUATE YOUR CURRENT PRODUCT
GATHER PRODUCT SALES DATA

Take a close look at your product sales. What product is selling and what isn't? What are the conversion ratios? There's more than one answer to each question—you can view sales data in multiple ways by reframing the angle. For example, you can look at your sales data based on the actual sale date, or the product delivery date. They are often the same date, but what if some products are not delivered because of cancellation? What are the actual sales in this case? That sales number is whatever number you choose to use as the basis for your decision-making, based on your priorities. You can use closed transactions to gauge company sales performance, or, if you're concerned only with actual revenues, you might use delivered sales as your framework.

Be flexible with your approach to data so you won't get boxed into the general conventions of a metric that doesn't give you the information you actually need. Establish key, relevant metrics to guide you.

This is a case where there really can be too much data. During a growth phase in one of my companies, we based our KPIs (key performance indicators) for an 85-inch TV screen on about two hundred different sets of company data. Discussions bounced from one metric to the next with no real direction. We couldn't get clarity. Finally, we realized we needed to operate with no more than three top-guiding metrics. All others would then be derivatives analyzed only after discovering any problems with any of the top three key metrics. This drill-down approach helped us reveal the information we needed to identify a specific problem and figure out how to fix it.

PUT YOURSELF IN THE MIND OF THE CONSUMER

To understand any problems that exist with your product, you really need to put yourself in the mind of the consumer. Forget what you currently know about the product and start from scratch. Imagine you're not a fan of your company or its product. Pretend this is the first time you've been made aware of it, and you have not been convinced that it's good enough to buy. At this point, you're simply considering the product. Be honest. What do you really think? What's making you want it and what's making you question it? Are you excited about the prospect of owning it? Or does the thought of buying it leave you emotionless?

Now, put yourself in the consumer's place and try to buy something from your company. Go to your company's website as a third party—not with your current profile—and try the different contact methods. Is there a phone number to call? Call it and see how long it takes someone to pick up. Or does it go to voicemail? If so, does someone call you back? How long does that take?

If there's an email address, send an email. If there's a contact form, fill it out. See how long it takes to get a response. See what kinds of results you get. You can take this experiment as far as you like, even through making a purchase, receiving the item, lodging a complaint, requesting customer service or support, and returning the item. Note how all your actions are handled. Did you experience any problems? Did you discover things your company could improve? All of that is invaluable information.

QUERY YOUR VENDORS

Talk to your vendor partners about your product. Many companies rely on their suppliers to provide them with key aspects of the product design because these people know what products are selling successfully. They can offer ideas and provide information about what is selling on the local, national, or world stage. There's a wealth of information to be had in these conversations.

You might have difficulty finding the time or the people to discuss these topics, but you need to make it happen. Identify those vendor partners you can easily connect with. You might be pleasantly surprised to find they will want to help you. Many times, it's as simple as that—they just want to help. Other times, they know if they help you with your product, they will be selling more to you, which is just as good as any other motive. After all, both of you are heading in the same direction. I've found many companies are able to make massive shifts in their product design and positioning simply by engaging in these kinds of conversations.

SURVEY YOUR CUSTOMERS

Focus groups and customer surveys can also help you get more information, although they require an investment of time and effort. Remember, no one can tell you more about how good your product is than your customers. Either they will buy your product, they already bought your product, or your product is being showcased to them, as in the context of a focus group. Whatever the situation, you'll come away from this conversation better informed about whether you are on the right track or need to change, add, or remove something from your product line.

FOLLOW ONLINE REVIEWS

Another product evaluation strategy is to pay attention to online reviews. What people are saying in public might reveal to you the big ideas consumers take away from your product offering, whether good or bad. You always have to take some reviews with a grain of salt, of course, because people's emotional reactions can be unreasonable. But if you keep an objective eye on what is being said, you will be able to read between the lines and see where the truth lies. Don't presume the best or the worst about information you are receiving and act on that faulty analysis. You want a realistic assessment.

ANALYZE INDUSTRY DATA

Every industry has publicly available data. It's your responsibility to follow the data, to make sense of it, and to gauge your product's performance relative to what the industry is doing. Knowing the state of the industry doesn't mean you must conform to the industry standard. In fact, your job is to exceed it, and you can only do that if you know where you stand. So, look at the data. You might analyze demographics, psychographics, and geographical locations of your typical consumer. You might ask questions only the data can answer, such as: How big is the market? Is it shrinking or growing? How does your product life expectancy and its price compare with competitors?

TALK TO YOUR PEOPLE

Talk to your people, especially your employees on the front lines. They know more about what needs to be done with your product than any consultant out there. Conduct these conversations in an environment where your employees feel comfortable talking with you. After all, you want them to be candid and not just tell you what they think you want to hear. Otherwise, any opinions you get will essentially be casual opinions, which could lead to ineffective decisions.

If you want to know what's wrong with a product, ask the people selling it; they know more about the customer than you. Ask them about their successes and failures. You may not get the answers you hoped to hear—in fact, your salespeople will most likely tell you everything they don't like about the product. If that happens, congratulate yourself, because you have created an environment where your sales team feels comfortable telling you the truth! Pay attention to their selling pains and what they're hearing from the consumer.

To get the most, and most useful, information, ask open-ended questions. But when you ask salespeople open-ended questions, you may open a floodgate of information, so be ready to receive it. If you seriously want to get maximum yield from this process, note any key concept or word they said that caught your attention. You will often discover insights that surprise you. For example, they may tell you that the problem they hear about most from others is not solvable by your product. Once you are aware of the discrepancy, you can devise a solution, incorporate it into your product, and thereby create additional products tailored to your customers.

To keep the insights coming, keep the dialogue going. In my experience, salespeople will not find it intrusive if you check in periodically. On the contrary, salespeople love to talk about the problems with a product they're trying to get out to the consumer. Their biggest fear is that no one is listening. If you listen, you will learn, and you can change things that need to be changed. In companies with flawed products, management may not realize the extent of the problem, but they still encourage the sales team to sell the flawed products, without seriously considering improving the product or addressing the issues the sales team faces with customers. If you want to succeed with your business, you should be continuously asking these questions and communicating your findings down the chain, and your employees should follow your example. People involved in selling are generally good listeners. They certainly know what customers are telling them. But you won't know that until you talk to them.

Salespeople are busy, and it's difficult to schedule regular time with them. And when you do finally talk, they may gloss over the big problems, because they already have too much to do. Besides, they may think that no one has listened to them in the past, so why would they be listened to now? Building trust takes time, so make a point of having an ongoing conversation with a few people in your sales department about a particular product or customer. In fact, you don't even have to talk about a specific product. Interesting and beneficial details can emerge from open-ended conversations.

For example, when one of your salespeople tells you a story about the customer who called constantly asking for clarifications about how to use the product, you might wonder if your customer service team is adequately equipped to give the correct instructions or if the written instructions are clear. Or you might hear about the customer who was so happy with what she could accomplish with the product that she recommended it to all of her colleagues. Whether the stories highlight good or bad things about your product, you glean important information. Armed with that information, you can amplify the good and solve the bad.

If you're unsure how to start these conversations, here are some helpful starters:

- What exactly is bothering your customers?
- What have you noticed is missing or needed?
- What do these observations suggest for new product ideas?
- What will solve customer problems or irritations about our product?
- If a solution within our company exists, does it offer a better result compared to what the competition offers?

CONSISTENTLY PRODUCE AN IMPROVED PRODUCT

With all the information you've gathered, you likely have some ideas about how your company's products can be improved—from product enhancements to better customer experiences. But where does the improvement actually happen? In many cases, product improvements come from within the ranks, from the team and employees charged with product improvement. But it goes beyond that. A continuously improving product requires involvement of both the team and the business owner or leader. As a business person, CEO, or high-level executive, you're not excused from the responsibility of innovating and continuously improving the product mix—even if it's not your sole responsibility.

Over the years, I've seen companies assign responsibility in three ways:

1. The CEO is 100 percent in charge.
2. The employees and teams are 100 percent in charge.
3. All work together hand in hand.

In general, I've found the third option to be the most effective. There are exceptions to the rule, but when all parties cooperate, that's when explosive results occur.

When you are in the Exit Mindset, you should be thinking about ways your company can turn out consistent product improvements with minimal input from you, and thus demonstrate that improvements will continue with minimal input from the new business owner, CEO, or other financial stakeholders. If you build teams and processes that can operate independently this way, potential buyers will recognize those as added value.

REPLACE YOURSELF

Starting with the right product for the right customers and creating a system for constantly improving on it not only adds value to your business, it allows you to meet your ultimate Exit Mindset goals: to gain time and increase freedom. And you can't have either unless you are profitable to the point that you can replace yourself in your business by having others do the things you do on a daily basis.

Replacing yourself sounds harsh, but it really comes down to bringing in the human resources needed to take over some of your responsibilities in exchange for financial compensation. This is how you're able to gain time and freedom. Think of it this way: Good product equals time and freedom. By creating an exit product, you're doing more than you probably thought possible—you're changing your life and your future for the better.

You must sometimes trust others to handle portions of the business. By all means, offer full training, provide handbooks, and communicate policies, but at some point you have to let go. I'm not asking you to take blind chances. If you find things aren't going well, then replace that resource or person. If all is well, then my guess is the price of your freedom is incalculable.

If you're reluctant to part with financial resources in exchange for someone else to take responsibilities from you, then you're being penny-wise but pound-foolish. Replacing yourself in the operation is the key to creating a bigger company that is scalable and has a higher valuation in the eyes of potential buyers. Scalability is a key to growth—you may be able to fill a hundred orders a day, but you won't be able to fill five hundred orders a day. Without help, you'll soon reach your limit.

DEMONSTRATE FUTURE DEMAND

A potential buyer of your company will want to know what the future of the business looks like. Oftentimes, the future is linked to present product strategy. If you're planning to exit the business, you may think that future demand is irrelevant to you—but realize that it is most certainly relevant to the buyer. Research the market to demonstrate and validate its future. If your market is shrinking, for example, you might need to figure out how to change your product or come up with a new one. As soon as you are sure the problem isn't a temporary one, immediate action is crucial.

Remember, the whole reason you're creating an exit business is so you can sell it for a high valuation, or keep it and have more time and a higher net worth. You won't be able to do either one if your product isn't sustainable. You need to project how many people will be entering the marketplace this year, next year, and ten years out. And then what percentage of that group will become your customers.

If you delay making these projections, you risk leaving your business stuck in the past, especially as the pace of technological change increases. The landscape can shift in the blink of an eye, and your company needs to be looking beyond the horizon. If it's not, the company won't be able to adapt. That might look like IBM pivoting way too slowly from mainframes to cloud technology, or software companies that didn't see the move to a subscription model (software-as-a-service) coming. Both missed out on many opportunities.

Even modest companies need to invest in research and development. We tend to think of R&D as something only big tech, manufacturing, and pharmaceutical companies do, but it applies to market research, too. Do your research and create a compelling picture of the product for yourself, your employees, stakeholders, and buyers. This isn't a product description—it's a reality-based vision of the future that allows the user to imagine what it's like to own your product.

In Silicon Valley, for example, most startup companies don't have a viable product they can take directly to market. In many instances, the product requires a great deal of further development. When one of those companies sells for exorbitant amounts of money, it's because of their product's potential, not where the product is at the time of the sale. That's precisely the position you want to be in: the position where someone comes to you because they can see how they might make a multiplier on the value you are selling. When this sort of deal goes through, both sides win. The buyer gets the potential, and you earn the higher reward.

CHAPTER 6 *EXERCISE*

Boosting an exit product's quality can elevate company valuation and selling price. Simultaneously, it benefits your company by creating products that align with consumer needs and drive profits. Consider these questions while shaping your exit product:

1 What is your product's purpose?

2 Have you ever wondered why your product lacks certain features? If yes, what action will you take to address this?

3 Is there anything you believe should be included in your product but is not yet? If yes, how will you integrate these features?

4 Do you wish anything about your product was different? If yes, what steps will you take to make these changes?

5 Have you noticed anything odd about your product? If yes, what measures will you take to understand or change this?

6 Are there additional features or enhancements you wish your product could offer? If yes, how will you work on incorporating them?

7 Do you think your product is missing any specific elements? If yes, what is your plan to add these features?

8 Is there a better or different way to approach your product? If yes, what actions will you take to implement this approach?

9 Are there specific modifications you are considering for your product? If yes, how will you put these changes into action?

FINAL STEPS TO AN EXIT PRODUCT

NOW THAT YOU'VE EVALUATED YOUR PRODUCT and pondered its future, do you think you're closer to an exit product? Even if the improvements are incremental, you're on the right track. The key to success is to make small steps in your modifications.

If you feel you're stalled, I can recommend a tactic used by one of the most successful companies in the world: The Walt Disney Company. It's called "Imagineering," which is defined as devising and implementing a new or highly imaginative concept or technology. Disney thinks this process is so important that they devote an entire Imagineering department to imagination and engineering to produce content.

So that's your assignment. Start by planning what your product could be and put together a plan with a timeline for creating it. This process will help you create a vision for your product that anchors everything else you do. Some people are natural visionaries, while others get bogged down in the process. It doesn't really matter which side you fall on. Simply envision what your product would look like if it were truly and effectively distinguished from other products. What would make it so different and so appealing that your market would proactively want it?

For now, imagine the best-case product. Don't limit your thinking. Don't focus on the obstacles, because all you will get is just that, obstacles! You're going to work through the details later, but for now I want you to practice the process that allows great products to be created, innovated, and sometimes even resurrected.

Consider July 20, 1969, when the United States landed two humans on the moon. This was a great feat, especially as the United States was way behind in the space race. Most people dismissed the possibility of going to the moon altogether; it was a wild idea not worthy of imagination. But somebody imagined it, and without that vision Neil Armstrong wouldn't have stepped foot on the moon's surface.

Throughout history, innovation has often followed on the heels of imagination. In the late 1800s, Alexander Graham Bell envisioned a device that allowed people to talk remotely, and Thomas Edison dreamed about a light that didn't require a candle flame or oil. A lot of work happened between those ideas and the ultimate inventions—the telephone and the incandescent lightbulb—but the work wouldn't have happened without the imagination to ask the right questions and seek the workable solution.

Granted, the rewards of creativity are seldom instant. Most inventions take many years and iterations before they actually work. Like Edison's lightbulb, your exit product may require ten thousand tries to get it right, but the long-term rewards are worth it. Think first about what you want your product to do. Then, try things. Don't worry about failing. You have room for that. Frankly, the cost of failure isn't as high as it used to be. You have the advantage of technologies and resources that make trial and error much more affordable than they were even just a few years ago. For example, you can take advantage of real-time global communications to lead your teams in this endeavor, and you can tap into a global talent pool for rapid prototyping and other work. You aren't limited by the resources and people currently under your roof.

Plus, you have the option to test your ideas long before you have to invest in production. Contemporary product design relies on prototypes, which are tested in a limited market. Once there's proof of concept, it can be further validated with market research before work begins on a final product ready for sale. For example, Google Ventures is well known for its "design sprint," where it prototypes its products prior to full deployment.

Finally, find a way to evaluate objectively. You might have a good product, but is it an exit product? Are you constantly involved with every small aspect of its creation? If that's the case, the process of product creation and modification is not scalable and self-running. Thus, you do not have an exit product.

CREATIVITY EXERCISES

To stir your creative faculties and ensure you're on to a winning idea, consider the following questions:

- Who should be using your product but is not? Why not?
- What are customers asking for that the competition doesn't offer?

- What if you borrow features of two or more product or service categories to create a new product?
- What trend in your subject area can you take advantage of?
- What if you take advantage of a national "mood" or reaction to a popular issue?
- What opportunities may be opened by social-political events now changing the world?
- What societal trends are becoming evident? What opportunities do they suggest?
- What opportunities are suggested by ecological/environmental change? What scientific or technical angle can you use?

ACQUIRE AND ADAPT

In addition to prototyping and developing an exit product, you can also acquire a product that complements what you have, and sell it as-is or configure it to better fit your own product. Large companies do this often. When Meta (previously Facebook) acquires a product, for example, it usually builds on the unique social portal concept the company grew from. It wants to acquire products that add functionality to its own portfolio. For example, Meta bought Instagram, WhatsApp, and Messenger, all purchases which augmented its core products. And of course, Meta has purchased many other companies and start-ups as well; it either left these apps as stand-alone products or integrated them into their platform.

Small- and medium-size companies can also acquire products. Even the smallest publishing company can acquire lines or titles and sometimes become a mid-sized powerhouse. A supplement vendor can acquire a manufacturing facility or a stand-alone competitor product. This is how many companies grow—through acquisition.

ROLL UPS AND JOINT VENTURES

There's one more way to grow rapidly—the "roll up." This concept was successful for a while in publishing companies, veterinary practices, and other industries where it is difficult to establish a nationwide presence. In a roll up, a group decides to acquire additional companies in the same space, and keeps on acquiring until they achieve their desired size or capitalization.

Alternatively, you can have a joint venture or a partial acquisition. The topic of joint ventures is too extensive to address comprehensively in this book, but I can offer some general advice. Each option you look at—whether it is to acquire and adapt, roll up, or undertake a joint venture—has its pros and cons. The main thing to consider is which option will help you expand your horizons to find ways you can broaden and improve your product.

For our purposes, we can say that whatever methods you choose, the goal is a product that's appealing to the customer and generates revenue. Remember, the sky's the limit and there are infinite possibilities. Don't limit yourself!

DIFFERENTIATING YOUR PRODUCT

If acquiring another company to enhance your product isn't an easily attainable objective at this time, there is a different path. You can create a differentiator product (a distinctive product that stands out in the market) by combining different products and services, eliminating features, creating a higher- or lower-end version, finding a different market, and so on.

COMBINE

The smartphone is the ultimate example of a combination of products. It's a phone, a networked computer, a camera, and a digital music player. Before the introduction of smartphones, these products were sold separately. If you needed to use all three together, you had to carry all three items with you. Combining them created a brand new product that does all three, in addition to performing many other functions we need and want.

The concept of a multifunctional smartphone seems obvious to us now, but in the early days of smartphone innovation, combining those products was a risky proposition. For example, if the concept for Apple's flagship product, the iPhone, had failed, Apple stock would have suffered, and that would have put the company in jeopardy. Apple executives knew it; they called the iPhone the "bet the company on it" device. All of us know now that they won that bet. But it was never a sure thing.

ELIMINATE

Many products became successful after eliminating an additional component or benefit in the product that was either a distraction or created inefficiency in the product objective. Remember the flip phone? When it became evident that a separate keypad wasn't necessary and could be replaced by a touch screen, the flip phone's days were numbered, at least in terms of functionality. There are still flip phones, but they are design choices, not operational ones.

DIFFERENTIATE

Many people who don't understand the concept of product positioning think their product is good for everyone in their general target consumer segment, in terms of construction, features, and quality. However, producing a variety of products to suit different needs and demographics has its place. Along with product differentiation, there is market differentiation. Either strategy can give you access to new audiences and bolster product sales.

Many companies produce differentiated versions of their products for different target segments. In many cases, your customers may already be looking for a differentiated version of your product. Maybe they're interested in paying less or don't need the higher-level version—in that case, you could offer a modified version with more economical features. Many large technology companies (computer manufacturers, for example) frequently release relatively more economical models to accommodate a wider market. While the less expensive versions embody quality and great features, they're still priced below the premium offering. With this strategy, the company can capture market share from its competitors and continue to sell their customers more products.

Differentiation works as long as the product fills a need that doesn't deliver anything below what the customer expects from reasonable use of your product. Don't cheapen it, dumb it down, or take important features away.

Market differentiation works differently but can still deliver good results. One way to differentiate target markets is to produce different upscale and mass-market products. For example, right now, the same company that owns the Hyatt hotels owns The Four Seasons hotels. Hilton owns more than one hotel brand as well, including the Residence Inn. Marriott owns many different brands, ranging from weekly economy to five-star international. Under those brands, Marriott can serve people who want premium and non-premium hotel rooms, depending on their needs and price point.

I advise you to use consumer data to determine potential markets rather than rely on your perceptions of people's preferences. Remember that a price point is not indicative of a consumer's wealth or status. There are many people of extreme wealth who are not willing to pay a premium. And there are many people of modest means attracted to premium products. Those looking for a more luxurious experience are willing to pay more. What dictates your product positioning is consumer demand, not your perceptions. Consumer data is the ultimate determinant of reality.

Consider, too, that a new market isn't always one looking for a specific product tier. Sometimes the market wants something different because its needs are different. Hotels usually cater to people who are passing through an area or flying in for a day or two. Another market exists for people who need a place to stay while they're vacationing or between permanent homes. The popularity of Airbnb showed there is a market for a non-hotel type experience. Private homeowners turned into mini-hotel owners, and satisfied that market by renting out apartments, condos, and houses to people by the night, the week, the month, or longer.

PICK YOUR PASSION

When you're trying to figure out your path to an exit product, consider your own passion as well. If you identify a product with great opportunity, but you don't care about it or don't want to be associated with it, then it's probably not the product for you.

While not a "must," it is always advisable to be in a line of business and product goods and services that appeals to you personally—at least what you're comfortable making, and better yet, excited to make. While it isn't critical for your passion to flow through to the buyer, it increases your engagement with the product's consumer in both tangible and intangible ways.

Choosing a product to champion is a different process for every one of us. You might be looking just for the profits a product generates regardless of whether you like it or not, or you may decide that some products aren't your style. I prefer to first choose what I'm interested in, cross it with potential profitability, and decide whether an opportunity exists.

EXAMINE THE PRODUCT JOURNEY

Products are rarely static; successful products are almost always the result of various iterations. Iterating sounds creative, and it is, but to do it well also requires discipline. Keep track of your product development process and be keenly aware of the small successes and failures along the way to an exit product. Look carefully at the history of your product in the organization. This will help you to see how you came up with the product in the first place. Go back to the history of your previous research and development. What went wrong as you developed the product, and what went right? Why is the product the way it is today?

Also, look at the product's past configuration and its success at the time. What prompted you to change it and what was the impact of those changes? Where do you see the product going in the future? Why do you think that? Is there competitive pressure to make changes/improvements? Does the marketplace look as though it is going in another direction? You must remain eagle-eyed and aware.

PLAN WITH AN EXIT TIMELINE IN MIND

So far in this chapter, we've talked about creative processes—from imagining the future to acquisitions and roll overs to creating targeted and differentiated products. But you can't just dream about these things and then leave the ideas out there—you have to make a plan for completion. If you don't assign a timeline for the process of creating your product or iterating an existing one, and specify a deadline for finishing it, you won't ultimately complete it, or it will take more time than is needed.

You might think your product is too complex for a timeline, but look at what companies creating incredibly sophisticated software do: they use timelines. They know that if they didn't have an end date in sight, they would never release a new product, because there are always improvements to be made in software. However, most software developers know they need to stop developing at some point and set a deadline for achieving at least the major objectives. Your product is no different. You need a plan and timeline to get it done.

SET AN END DATE

Start with a list of your current products and another list of potential products you want, then combine the two lists. Filter the combined list to a manageable, realistic product line, and then set up a deadline to accomplish that objective. It's simple enough to get started: Choose the date it will be a reality and figure out what has to happen between now and then to meet that date.

CREATE MILESTONES

Milestones or guideposts are critical measures of your progress. If you only set one deadline for an entire project, you won't know until the end of the project if you finished on time, finished early, or were six months late. So, once you have a definitive outline of all the steps you will take to create/recreate an exit product, then you must set a deadline date for each one.

SCHEDULE SPECIFIC STEPS

Within each milestone, you can set out even more specific schedules. For example, if milestone three is "write new code to allow customers access to the product," you will need to find someone to do the coding. This necessitates another milestone in between: "hire or contract for a coding person to do the work." If you know it will take a week or more to hire that person, and you've set a deadline of one week for the entire coding step, you can now see that your schedule isn't reasonable, and you'll be forced to adjust other milestones to reflect that. We all want to get things done quickly, but there is little or no use in setting amazing deadlines when you know you don't have a chance of meeting them. Be reasonable, yet push yourself.

ACKNOWLEDGE THE UNKNOWNS

Creating a timeline seems like a nice, neat, linear process, but it is rarely that easy. For any project with any degree of complexity, something can and will go wrong. In my years of doing this, I've found that Murphy's Law doesn't fail often. In fact, it is a surprise when things do go according to plan.

Alternatively, you can follow the warfare axiom that states, "No plan survives contact with the opponent." In other words, no matter how well you plan a battle, something will go differently than you expect. This reality should be factored into your planning—always consider that there will be unknown variables. Build some contingency into your schedule to accommodate this.

TACTICS AND STRATEGIES TO IMPLEMENT AN EXIT PRODUCT

With all of this planning as your foundation, you will ultimately reach the point where you have to make it real—the moment of active deployment to the marketplace. This is the moment when action is taken, results can be observed, and course corrections can be made.

Some people do a lot of thinking, then stall at deployment. They have many great ideas and may even have a plan, but they never execute it. Some of that can be attributed to human psychology—the human brain tends to focus on upcoming pain and turn it into a boogeyman. It tricks you into a state of fear so you think that deployment will be difficult and painful and should be avoided. It's a built-in self-defense mechanism to protect you from anything that could cause discomfort.

However well-meaning the brain's intention, you must rise above the fear. There will be pain, and that's okay. Good things can happen despite the pain, but they never happen because we avoid the pain. Consider the people whose accomplishments you admire most—imagine all the difficulties they went through to achieve what they did. They didn't do it without some pain.

Focus on your ultimate Exit Mindset goal. You want a product that generates greater profits, increases company valuation, and gives you more time to pursue other interests. You must have known at some level that there would be work involved.

Here it is—the difficult, painful work. Don't worry, though; it's not that bad. You've already done the tough part. You've *thought* about it, and thinking is often the most difficult work.

FOLLOW THE FEEDBACK LOOP

Okay, you have a product deployment plan in mind, and you have decided how you want to proceed. Now, before you do anything, revisit the process you followed to get there from the beginning. Go over every element, including market research, product evaluation, and anything else that sparked your interest in this chapter and made its way into your plan. Start from the beginning, make adjustments where called for, and move forward. You can't reach your exit product in a linear way because some of your later changes will impact your planning decisions. Stop at every change and every decision you make and look back to see if something else needs to change. Follow this procedure to redefine your plan, and repeat the procedure during the actual deployment. Take a step back and see the results. Are they what you expected? Does something at an earlier stage in the plan need to change? Evaluate the results of every stage and capture any new information. Use it to make your plan and deployment better.

I call this process an iterative feedback loop. I want you to use it to make adjustments to ensure you're making the product you set out to make. You must continue to take the pulse of your consumer market, too, and make sure that what you started out to make still makes sense within it. Consumer sentiment is a moving target, and the iterative feedback loop is the process that prevents you from ending up with the wrong product.

I told you before that product is king. I'm saying it again because it's a critical reminder. You can, of course, have a product—many products—and have a business, work hard, earn great income, and have a life without living by this principle. But what you may not have is a saleable business. If you want to help yourself, your employees, and the consumer, keep creating better products. You'll be helping the world, too, because the world needs better products.

CHAPTER 7 _EXERCISE_

To stay productive and focused on the end goal while developing an exit product, contemplate the following questions:

What product enhancements do customers request and why? If any, what steps will you take to address these needs?

What elements of your product do customers dislike and why? How will you adjust those features?

Which competitive products do customers prefer and why? What actions will you take to compete?

What product misperceptions exist and why? How will you correct these misunderstandings?

What positive product perceptions need reinforcing? What strategies will you use?

What aspects of your product are inconvenient or unsuitable, and why? What changes will you implement?

What mistakes do customers make using your product? How can you make it more user-friendly?

What aspects of your product should remain unchanged?

If changes could alienate customers, how will you mitigate this risk?

Can you revitalize your product without actual changes, perhaps through marketing? If yes, what strategies will you employ?

Could improvements come from marketing innovation rather than product enhancement? If so, what marketing strategies will you adopt?

What do salespeople/suppliers/distributors suggest about market needs and your product's shortcomings? How will you respond to this feedback?

Where should you focus product improvement efforts for the highest ROI/effectiveness? What steps will you take in these areas?

PART THREE

EXIT INFRASTRUCTURE

DEVELOPING YOUR EXIT INFRASTRUCTURE

IN·FRA·STRUC·TURE: THE BASIC PHYSICAL AND organizational structures and facilities needed for the operation of a society or enterprise.

When most people hear the word "infrastructure," they think about bridges and roads. But in this chapter, we'll look at a different kind of infrastructure—business infrastructure. While the word has an undeserved reputation as being overly complex and confusing, for our purposes, I've simplified the concept for you.

To build a company that is scalable, self-running, and potentially more valuable when you sell it or otherwise exit, you must first build a self-running, scalable infrastructure—an **exit infrastructure**. Without an exit infrastructure, your exit product (and your company) will not achieve its optimal valuation point.

Developing an exit infrastructure is one of the most difficult tasks in developing and growing a company—not to mention it's the main factor in creating a sound business in the first place. Yet most business owners struggle with this task because of the sheer number of actions they need to carry out to create a successful operational framework for their company. In this chapter, I use a four-part model to make your job easier, customizable to your own situation.

EXIT INFRASTRUCTURE = SLPP

Think of infrastructure as the internal organs of your company. Each part works with the other parts to meet the common objective of developing, producing, and delivering a product that the consumer wants, ensuring the survival and growth of your company. Without the right infrastructure, your company teeters on chaos—a disaster waiting to happen. But if you create the right internal architecture, your company will thrive and potential buyers of your company will pay more attention to what you have and be more willing to pay the right price for buying your company.

I encourage you to follow a four-part model I call SLPP. It focuses on four elements that you can fix and develop with an Exit Mindset, allowing you to realize significant increases in the valuation of your company and moving you closer to your goal: increasing your profits, time, and freedom.

SLPP incorporates the following elements:

- Systems
- Locations
- Processes
- People

Granted, these aren't all of the elements that comprise a company's framework. The SLPP model isn't intended to describe every detail of what infrastructure entails. Instead, it focuses on those pieces that make the most difference from the perspective of an Exit Mindset. If you pay attention to these four important pieces, you'll take care of your company's worst infrastructure problems.

S IS FOR SYSTEMS

Your company consists of multiple systems that must seamlessly work with each other. I define *system* as an arrangement of interdependent groups, parts, and workflows that operate in a manner that creates a consistent, replicable, and scalable outcome. Further, a system can be made of subsystems that help lead to the outcome the master system is designed to achieve.

Consider the automobile. Your automobile is a master system that consists of many subsystems that lead to one outcome: transporting you from one location to another. You take for granted that your automobile will get you to your destination as long as it doesn't have mechanical defects or is in need of repair. The system is so well constructed that under normal circumstances, you don't have to worry about it. Examples of subsystems within an automobile are the engine, exhaust system, cooling system, and steering system. Each of the automobile's subsystems is complex, but they are designed to work together seamlessly as one unit.

Think of your business in the same way. Can it run in such a way that you can count on it to produce the exact same outcome every time? Or is your business more like a car that is prone to break down and is simply unreliable? Is your business model cohesively constructed? Or is it an ad hoc combination of systems, some or all of which will break down in some way at some time?

A business with well-planned and constructed systems is a business that's more easily exited than one that's chaotic without clearly defined and implemented systems. Even if you never exit the business, having efficient, scalable systems will help you generate higher profits and give you more time for other pursuits.

L IS FOR LOCATIONS

Locations are where your company operates. It's the area, facility, or space where specific parts of your company's operations and systems are conducted. Locations can be physical, virtual, or a combination of both, and they tend to be reference points by which others associate you with your business.

P IS FOR PROCESSES

Without processes, your business will be in chaos. A process is a set of instructions designed to guide people and equipment into producing a definable outcome. Some people confuse systems with processes, but they are different. In our automobile example, the system will always function in the same order, but the processes the driver uses to navigate will vary depending on the situation. Processes can be invoked when needed, while systems operate exactly the same way all of the time.

In business, a process allows you to fulfill a certain request as the need arises, building flexibility into your business. Using processes creates a more efficient and scalable infrastructure. By eliminating chaos and allowing management and employees to plan for resource use, processes affect profits by allocating resources efficiently. The right processes can make a dramatic improvement in your company's operations.

P IS FOR PEOPLE

Regardless of what your company does, its people are its biggest asset. There's no such thing as a company that doesn't need people. Even if you're selling something that's fully automated, you need someone to design and maintain that automation. You need people to modify and improve it. You need people to think about what to do next when the market changes and your product needs to adapt.

Most often, however, business owners need people to build the company's infrastructure. "People" doesn't just mean your employees and independent contractors; it also means your vendors, suppliers, and anyone else you need to maintain your company. Having quality people on your team is key to creating your exit infrastructure and is an attractive asset to potential buyers. If you implement a strong "people" infrastructure, you'll be able to create a better business model, and that will set the stage for your Exit Mindset.

AN OPTIMAL INFRASTRUCTURE STARTS WITH SLPP

You can look at SLPP as the chassis that makes your business functional. Product may be king, but product starts with an idea, and it's a proper SLPP that turns that idea into an exit product.

Before Henry Ford's vision of an assembly line system, automobile manufacturing operated under a craft production model, which involved making one vehicle at a time. Each part was made by hand or by machine, and then people put the parts together to make the automobile. That infrastructure didn't give the business owner freedom or financial leverage because of its reliance on each individual craftsman and their specialty in the production process.

Some manufacturers persisted with the craft model as long as they could. For many years after Ford began mass production, Rolls Royce continued producing one car at a time, at great expense and, thus, at great cost to its customers. While they were touted as the best motorcars on the market, over 99 percent of the public could not afford to buy one.

In 1908, the Ford Model-T led the way in mass production. Mass production was more efficient than craft production back then and has gotten even more so. The process continues to evolve. For instance, when Toyota extensively employed an improvement in the manufacturing process called "just-in-time" (JIT) manufacturing, where automobiles were built with parts that arrived just in time for assembly, that innovation helped Toyota become one of the largest automobile manufacturers in the world. Now, "lean" manufacturing processes are used in a variety of industries throughout the world.

These are examples of the evolution in infrastructure design in large automobile companies, but the lessons apply to us all: Every company must pay attention to its internal architecture. Even if you have a small operation, don't believe for a minute that you don't need infrastructure planning—you do! Your plan doesn't have to be like everyone else's, but you must have one, and you must stick to it to succeed. Just be sure to always be on the lookout for refinements and improvements.

Companies that adopt mass production practices aren't all the same—each company tailors how it frames its work according to its needs—but they still have a lot in common. They must figure out a way to break down the individual tasks required to build a product and assign multiple people to each task. That was Ford's breakthrough thinking that birthed the modern assembly line. You will find the assembly line architecture in even the simplest operations, such as fast-food, where it changed the nature of the restaurant industry. It was that infrastructure that attracted Ray Kroc to buy the business from the McDonald brothers. That's the power of infrastructure. It's instrumental in creating an exit strategy.

AN EXIT INFRASTRUCTURE INCREASES VALUATION

Either you have an exit infrastructure, or you don't, and most business owners don't. Like the best-designed business frameworks, an exit infrastructure creates the company's product and gets it into the hands of consumers in the most effective and efficient way. The company's entire framework is oriented toward producing that result. An exit infrastructure is scalable, moveable, expandable, and sellable. It can be an instrument to generate higher revenues, create more time, and lay the groundwork for the increasing valuation of your business.

Analyzing infrastructure can be a challenge, especially if you didn't start out accounting for future scaling or for selling your business. If so, you're not alone. Most other business owners didn't start out with these things in mind. You can meet that challenge now, or you can let the buyer of your company pay a lower price for your business and capitalize on the infrastructure gap opportunity. If you want to be the one making the profit and the higher valuation, you'll need to create an infrastructure that's scalable, expandable, and sellable at maximum value. In developing an Exit Mindset, when it comes to infrastructure, your first step is to examine and evaluate, carefully and methodically, how your current business framework functions.

THE IMPACT OF EXIT INFRASTRUCTURE

Working within a poorly constructed infrastructure is a lot of work. When your business has an infrastructure that doesn't take your exit into consideration, you're constantly walking into a host of problems. These problems are unpredictable, frequent, and seemingly random—trouble can pop up in any department and at any level. These problems could be anything from a resource shortage to an employee shortage to a vendor not delivering what you need. You might have to deal with a breakdown in hardware or issues with software. Or maybe you have to resolve issues among employees, between departments, or between your people and vendors.

These infrastructure issues constantly impact production. You know this costs money, and you know it's way too hard to reach the goals you've set. Every issue requires your attention. Instead of being the business leader, you're the problem fixer. You're constantly putting out fires. That leaves no time for strategy. If you do find time to strategize, the constant issues make it almost impossible to predict your future. How can you organize your time and efforts with any confidence when you're mired in day-to-day issues and problems?

With an exit infrastructure, your situation dramatically changes. You settle into your office, and it's quiet. No one is bringing a problem to your door. Everything runs smoothly. That's not to say you won't have to fix major issues from time to time, but problem-solving is no longer the day-to-day and minute-by-minute function you perform. Now you're the leader. You're the strategist. You study, research, and investigate your business, your industry, and the market. You identify the risks, challenges, and opportunities. And you define the next destination and direct the company on a path to get there. Your hard work is paying off with profits—tangible proof that you're doing it right.

A strong infrastructure benefits all who have a stake in the success of your company. It impacts your freedom as a business owner and the freedom of your employees. It impacts your company's finances and your employees' finances. It impacts your suppliers, your community, and the economy as a whole.

The impact of an exit infrastructure on the people who work inside the business and keep it running is especially substantial. Think of your workers as some of your major stakeholders, since their growth hinges on the success of the company. A good infrastructure leads to a productive company where people want to work. The culture is better because there's more predictability. Everyone knows how things work, and they understand their roles. They don't have to worry about you constantly checking in on them, because you're busy working on strategy, not micromanaging them.

A strong exit infrastructure, incorporating all four elements of SLPP, makes your business more resilient and able to respond more quickly to unexpected challenges. Exit infrastructure is also key to achieving a higher valuation that can lead to a good exit.

INFRASTRUCTURE FROM THE BUYER'S POINT OF VIEW

Just as you're trying to create more value in your company, potential buyers of your company are trying to place a value on your business. To do this, they will carefully investigate your products, infrastructure, and customer conversation. When they look at the infrastructure, they wonder whether they will have to make an investment in it, how much of an investment they will have to make, and what the bottom-line impact of that investment will be on the company's value. Importantly, they want to know if solid production relies on the owner of the company or key executives remaining with the business.

The reason this is top of mind for buyers is that, as previously mentioned, many companies depend so heavily on the owner or a key executive that they cease to function when that person leaves. That's the downfall for many small- and even medium-size businesses. To avoid joining their ranks, make sure that multiple people are capable of maintaining a very high standard of production for your exit product. This might mean divulging some closely held information, but any employee smart enough to take on such responsibility will figure it out anyway. You might as well have them on your side in the event of an emergency.

Company buyers know that hidden infrastructure problems are common, so they do their due diligence to uncover such issues. They want as much information as they can gather about the product, the demand for the product, and the company's ability to produce it in a cost-effective way that generates profits. The buyer of your company also wants to know whether they will have to be involved in running the business on a day-to-day basis and how many problems they will be facing. Don't attempt to hide potential issues. Most buyers will find ways to uncover the truth, and those who can't will likely take you to litigation for withholding the information.

There *are* certain instances where buyers take on companies with poor infrastructures. They intentionally invest money in them because they have concluded that the product is so great it's worth the risk, effort, and expense. This is common in large companies purchasing start-ups where the operation isn't that good, but the product is. But any product worth that risk has to be pretty outstanding.

So, what if you have a product that's not 100 percent fantastic, but your company has an excellent infrastructure in place to deliver it? In other words, what if the intrinsic value of your company lies in its infrastructure? Better yet, what if your company has the infrastructure to improve the product and get it to the right customer? If any of these scenarios describes your company, you may have a higher valuation based on that fact alone, and thus the basis for asking for a higher price. A savvy buyer of your company might pick up on that and be willing to pay for it.

After evaluating its architecture, value your company accordingly. Companies with infrastructures designed to create maximum leverage have a higher valuation and are offered at a premium. The buyer may initially consider the price too high, but in the long run they will see it's worth it because they won't be stuck trying to figure out how to fix the company's orientation and framework. If you want a company that you can sell for a premium, build the infrastructure to support it.

HOW DIFFERENT BUYERS VIEW INFRASTRUCTURE

To evaluate your current infrastructure, put yourself inside the buyer's head. What are they thinking? You have to be totally objective in your view, which is harder than you think. Most business owners think their business is in better shape than it really is. Only through critical evaluation will you discover what the buyer sees. In Chapter 1, I told you about the three types of buyers: flippers, integrators, and participants. All three types are interested in your infrastructure and how well it's designed and working at the time you exit.

Most buyers are flippers. You could also think of them as investors. They want to profit from the business without actually working in the business. Some investors may not be interested in the details of the infrastructure, but they still want to know how well it works. Their objective is to figure out whether the company can be profitable the way it currently operates. If the infrastructure isn't up to standard, their ability to be profitable could be compromised, and that will substantially affect their valuation. Alternatively, they might consider buying your business and improving the infrastructure so they can either keep it and have higher profit margins or sell it for a markup.

Buyers who are integrators are also interested in your infrastructure, but to a lesser degree than investors. They have an infrastructure at their existing business. If your company's infrastructure can easily integrate into their own, their valuation might be higher.

The third type of buyer—the participant—will be the most concerned with the infrastructure. They'll be dealing with it day in and day out. Ideally, they want a business they can just step into with no major investment of their time, money, or energy.

Knowing the impact of business architecture, isn't it worth it to you to improve your company's infrastructure yourself? You've put years of your life into building your business—why not make the improvements necessary to sell it for a higher value instead of letting the buyer get all the benefits of what you built over the years?

DESIGNING YOUR INFRASTRUCTURE FOR SCALABILITY

The best businesses are scalable, and scalability is a function of infrastructure design. The better your design, the easier it is to expand your business and the easier it is to achieve higher valuation for your company. Bottlenecks are the biggest obstacles to designing a good infrastructure. Of course, we can't dismiss the importance of processes, great leadership, good execution, and other factors; however, a system can only run as fast as its slowest component, and that's what bottlenecks are.

Let me give you an example: If you take a race car and install spark plugs that limit the car to fifty miles per hour, your race car won't win any races. It will break down as soon as it goes past fifty miles per hour, even though it's otherwise well-designed, just because of one suboptimal component. Your company operates similarly. No matter how well designed, it can't pass through infrastructure bottlenecks any quicker than those bottlenecks allow.

Make yourself an expert at identifying bottlenecks. Examine your company's processes and infrastructure, ask questions, and make observations from a high-level perspective. Sometimes, bottlenecks can be hard to fix, but in many cases, identifying them is more than half the battle—they become easier to solve once you identify them.

Solutions are easier said than done, of course. Most of the time, your team is busy. Asking them to resolve a bottleneck by giving them more work when their plates are already filled will create some pressure on them. Sometimes, your people will resist. They might tell you that the innovative changes you want to make won't work. You may be told that your plans are simply beyond the capacity of the human resources available.

You don't have to give up at that point. And you don't have to insist that your plan be implemented no matter what. Instead, negotiate timelines and expectations, and enter a dialogue about how the plan aligns with your team leaders and relevant employees. Involving others will help you gain willing cooperation and commitment, which will go a long way toward resolving the bottleneck.

Keep your sights focused on what's important. If your goal

is to expand the business, you can get there more quickly with an exit infrastructure. If you can demonstrate seamless scalability to a prospective company buyer, they will place a higher value on your business. When you're selling your business, the highest premium lies in your company's future potential. The ability to scale your company demonstrates future potential to a buyer without requiring them to make a major investment or expend extraordinary effort.

A franchise is a perfect example of a scalable infrastructure. The franchisor has designed a business that a franchisee can step into because its infrastructure is seamless and scalable. The franchisor doesn't have to be involved in the day-to-day operations and, in many cases, neither does the franchisee.

Subway, for example, replicates the same basic infrastructure at every location. There may be slight variations, but a Subway in Milwaukee is almost identical to one in San Diego. The two stores have different employees, but they work in similar roles. There could be something on the menu in one shop that the other shop doesn't carry because of the location and local tastes, but they're both run by the same handbook. They follow the same procedures for baking the bread and making the sandwiches. The whole operation is so clearly defined that the business owner can train other people to run a Subway so he doesn't have to be there every day.

Have you ever been to a restaurant where the owner is always there? They don't dare take a week off because they fear the place would fall apart if they did. A franchise owner isn't in that position. Any successful business with multiple locations has figured out how to build an exit-able, scalable, repeatable infrastructure. Eateries like Subway, Starbucks, and The Cheesecake Factory are all scalable, but the concept isn't limited to the restaurant industry. If you want to build a true exit infrastructure, it pays to take a close look at how these businesses operate.

THE IMPACT OF EXIT INFRASTRUCTURE ON COMPANY FINANCIALS

A chaotic infrastructure is a constant drain on company financials. When you have to spend extra time and effort to accomplish something that you might have otherwise been able to do less expensively, you're working against your company's success. With a poor business architecture, you can't leverage people, processes, hardware, software, or real estate in a way that could save you money and create more revenue.

An ineffective infrastructure also hampers your ability to predict financial events and correlates to decreases in future profits. Deliverables end up being costlier to complete, whether because of excess payroll or other factors. Maintaining a low-grade infrastructure is much more expensive than maintaining a scalable, efficient one. Inefficiencies in this area create opportunity costs, too. If you don't have a good infrastructure that's scalable, growth is limited. Any revenues you didn't make because of unnecessary infrastructure oversights are losses to you—these are the phantom losses discussed in Chapter 4.

Take, for example, a company with $10 million in revenues. It could be making $20 million with a better infrastructure, but has not made internal changes that would bring revenues to $20 million. This perspective comes as a revelation to people who ask me how to improve their revenues. You should always account for phantom losses. In this case, what you don't see will hurt you.

THE GIFT THAT KEEPS GIVING

One company I'm familiar with generates about 20 to 30 percent profit and $60 million a year in revenues. The owners started this business several years ago and poured their lives into it. When they wanted to sell it, they were approached by private equity firms. The potential buyers liked the business a lot—it had a good product, a good conversation going with the consumer, and the infrastructure practically ran itself. The owners were pretty excited about the enormous amounts of money they were set to make from the deal.

But the more they thought about it, the more the owners realized they had a really good thing going. They had built a machine that was churning out profits year after year and could continue doing so for years to come. They loved the business, the lifestyle it gave them, and the freedom it provided. After more consideration, they decided not to sell. That's the kind of freedom a solid exit infrastructure can give you. Some business owners with exit infrastructures that are profitable and fun to run do sell, of course, but not until they really want to. Some want to move on to start another business. Others want to retire. But none are just trying to get out from under a business that's weighing them down. That's the power and flexibility you get from the Exit Mindset.

Those who didn't build an exit infrastructure, on the other hand, often sell because they are exhausted. The business starts to be a grind, and they just want out. And since those business owners didn't do what was necessary to achieve a higher valuation, they end up selling their business for whatever they are offered, which is usually a low price compared to all the effort they put in to build it over the years. The sad reality here is that, at this point, the seller really doesn't care what they get for the business. They just want out. And the buyer doesn't care how much work the first owners put into it. The buyer only cares about what the company can do for them from a future revenue perspective and the work and resources they have to put into it to achieve their objectives.

An exit infrastructure is crucial to developing your Exit Mindset. Creating and implementing one is both an art and a science. You must integrate your systems, location, processes, and people (SLPP) in a manner that creates scalability and improves your company's financial standing, but you can't do it by introducing a robotic process or relying on a software program. Designing an optimized, high-value business architecture requires more than science; it requires the intangible elements of your own thinking and awareness.

CHAPTER 8 *EXERCISE*

While assessing your company's structure, consider these questions:

1
What actions are required for your product's market introduction? If necessary, what is your action plan?

2
Which parts of your infrastructure function optimally and why?

3
Does your infrastructure consistently produce the expected outcome? If not, what will you do to improve it?

4
Is your business model well-integrated? If changes are needed, what will you implement?

5
Do daily issues frequently demand your time and focus? How will you manage them effectively?

6
Where do frequent issues arise across your enterprise's departments? What is your strategy to mitigate these?

7
Have you evaluated your infrastructure from a potential buyer's perspective? If not, what are your plans to transition to an exit infrastructure?

EXIT INFRASTRUCTURE IN ACTION

BECAUSE YOUR COMPANY'S INFRASTRUCTURE is a system of components working together for a greater whole, it's important to see each piece and optimize it. This relates to the principle of the slowest component determining the speed of the whole. Most business owners have a hard time conceptualizing that their company infrastructure has discrete components. A major reason for this is that it's common in companies to have many people performing multiple functions. For example, somebody working in operations might also be involved in human resources, blurring the line between the functional units. Often, just a few people manage multiple jobs or multiple functions, and most of those functions aren't clearly defined. This makes it very difficult to unpack the components of infrastructure.

If you can't see it, you can't fix it, and unless you take stock from a high-level perspective, company infrastructure problems are likely to remain hidden. In today's evolved business environment, you can't afford to make such a mistake—every time you have to decide about what problem to tackle, your attention drifts from focusing on the strategic picture. That's why owners often fall into the habit of dealing with detail after detail—they can see incremental progress, even when the big-picture strategy doesn't make sense. Your mission from today on is to change that.

You can reach this higher-level perspective by quantifying your infrastructure, understanding it, and then creating a visual map of it. I recommend using a mind-mapping tool for this job in order to illustrate the connections and relationships among the structural components. And don't forget that the people of your company are a large part of this structural mapping.

BREAK YOUR COMPANY INTO PARTS

Most companies have three structural tiers in terms of people: upper management, mid-level management, and the people on the front lines. It might be difficult for you to envision these units when your company is small, but no matter the size of your business, you almost certainly have structural tiers. Even if you don't have people in highly segmented teams, you can still think departmentally. When you start thinking that way, you can start building the units that make sense for your company's operation. These units might include marketing, sales, research and development, etc. Once you have your list, identify or assign who should be in charge of each unit.

One way to help you visualize this process is to think about each department as a separate company that produces an output contributing to the final outcome of the mother company. Each internal "microcompany" produces a part of the whole. To create a good exit product, you need to develop an efficient infrastructure that helps these microcompanies work together to assist in the creation of that product.

In a small business, you, as the CEO, might also be accountable for many units, in addition to being the person accountable and responsible for ensuring the company architecture is scalable and optimized for an exit. Don't let those responsibilities deter you from pressing on with the objective of developing an exit infrastructure. At some point, you will replace yourself in those positions. Each replacement takes you one step closer to a solid and saleable exit.

Let's go back to the McDonald's example to help you visualize the necessary shift in perspective. Historically, restaurants had one person create each sandwich (or other menu item). The McDonald brothers, however, wanted to create an infrastructure for mass producing a burger faster and more efficiently. They had an idea, but it was so new they weren't sure if it could work. To test it out, they went into an open area and started drawing lines on the ground representing each station. Then, they simulated moving among the stations, even though there were no grill tops or counters in front of them. If you had looked at them from far away, you probably would have been baffled by their behavior. But they knew what they were doing: they were trying to understand whether a particular configuration of stations would create efficiency from an infrastructure standpoint. That simple exercise led to a revolution in the fast-food industry.

Try to approach every aspect of product creation from an infrastructure perspective. Return to SLPP by superimposing your systems, locations, processes, and people on your product cycle. If part of your operation is to process a certain amount of paperwork, use the SLPP model to see where you could make changes to improve the yield. Following this process will help you make decisions about how to reconfigure that part of the infrastructure to make it more powerful and productive.

This is another instance when working back to front can provide big benefits. Start with your final product in mind and work backward. Instead of focusing on the people and their roles, look at what actually happens to create an output. How is that product made? What are the steps? Thinking about your business this way reveals the weaknesses you need to address and the opportunities you can harness to improve your infrastructure. If you take that thinking to every part of your company, you will eventually get to your desired exit infrastructure.

All this doesn't need to be complicated; it's a mindshift, a different way of seeing your business. For instance, you might think that your small business doesn't have a manufacturing component because most people don't relate manufacturing to smaller, highly specialized operations. That's a mistake, because for every company, small or large, there's a degree of manufacturing that goes on, with or without machinery. Take Uber, for example. The company doesn't have a factory, yet they manufactured a combined set of processes, data, and people using a specific technology infrastructure to produce one product called a "ride." They manufactured it in such a way that the market saw it as distinct. Therefore, you must think of your business, your unit, or your division as a manufacturer of a product or service.

Obviously, manufacturing and products go hand in hand. It's impossible to have a product without manufacturing capability; to have something to sell to your customers, you have to manufacture it. The question is: Is that manufacturing capability scalable or sellable? Or is it reliant on other systems that are notably weaker and won't escape a potential buyer's notice? Whether your company employs a large number of people or just one, you can look at exit infrastructure this same way.

William Hewlett and David Packard provide a good example. They started a company in a garage, and from those humble beginnings built the Hewlett-Packard company. To reach that mark, they had to think about their infrastructure and how to grow it, scale it, and ultimately how to arrive at an exit infrastructure. Imagine if they hadn't! Their company would have landed in the ranks of the unknowns, along with all of the other companies that never tried to look at the product, infrastructure, and conversation from an exit perspective, as you're looking at your company right now.

Even a one-person shop can, and should, look at its infrastructure this way. You might think that a freelance writer, for example, doesn't have a product. That's actually not true. The product is the final manuscript, which can be published or sold privately. That's a product, no different than any other in the marketplace. And the writer's tools and systems are the infrastructure required to produce that manuscript.

Regardless of your product, you have to ask, What do those infrastructure units that produce the product look like, and are they efficient, productive, and scalable? What can I do to make them more efficient, productive, and scalable?

When you look at each unit, how it operates, and the output it produces, ask yourself if it can produce more by adding people. Scalability doesn't mean that by adding a person, the company benefits only from the additional labor. Rather, scalability means that adding the right person allows the entire unit to increase its output in a holistic way. Scalability applies to more than people, as well; it also means systems, locations, and processes that are combined to create a synergistic effect. An infrastructure that relies heavily on people alone is hard to scale. Yet, adding to any of the SLPP factors in a way that increases output for the operating unit is a positive thing and should not be ignored, even if it's more labor. Evaluate and design all units of your infrastructure to produce this effect.

FINANCIAL INFRASTRUCTURE

Is your company financially healthy? Do you have the right funds allocated to the right units? Are you meeting your financial benchmarks? Can the cash flow support the company? Let's consider those questions from the perspective of a financial infrastructure.

You have to allocate cash resources to the right infrastructure units so you can get a justifiable ROI on each unit. This might mean diverting revenue toward improvements. The trick is, you have to balance growth with maintaining a strong financial position. This can be difficult because there's always risk involved when you make changes to your business. You want to ensure you're efficient and profitable enough that you don't run into financial trouble. But, at the same time, you want to make sure you have funds allocated to other venues of revenue and R&D so you don't get left behind because your operations aren't scalable. It's a balancing act requiring the attention of financial experts who can help you map out a strategy. Any potential buyer of your company will pay close attention to your financial statements. You should get there first.

If your company is of a certain size, coordinating between the CEO and the Chief Financial Officer (CFO) is one way to achieve balance. Usually, the CFO is in charge of saving money, while the CEO is in charge of spending money. When you balance the two, things work out very well. Pay attention to one side more than the other, however, and you're in for potential trouble.

For example, if the CEO has an incredible vision for building and scaling the company, but is spending in a manner that doesn't lend itself to good fiscal responsibility, as the CFO sees it, then your company can hit some serious obstacles to its operations. Your CFO, on the other hand, is an expert in financial management but not in building and scaling companies—it's simply not their mindset or job. Their job is to make sure you don't go on a wild tangent. Of course, your CEO and CFO might not agree on the definition of "tangent."

Look at your company as if it were a car, with a gas pedal and brake pedal. Typically, as the CEO, you're pushing the gas; you have to burn cash to grow. Your CFO is like your brake. He or she is there to tell you when to stop or slow down. You should listen to their advice as you strategically deem appropriate. Consider them a friendly adversary.

In some scenarios, you might be acting as both CFO and CEO of your company, operating with both of your feet. Sometimes you'll have to push the gas and the brakes at the same time, powering forward while simultaneously putting the brakes on some of your financial initiatives. You can make that work, but it's exhausting. The key here is balancing fiscal responsibility and risk assessment. If you have those two covered, you're in for a smooth ride.

UNDERSTAND YOUR RISK

At every step of infrastructure development, you must understand the probabilities of every action you take and the consequences associated with those probabilities. Gaining that knowledge is called risk assessment.

To assess risk, look at any given proposition and determine the probability of success. Assuming that it could fail, what would happen? Will your business be in jeopardy, or just suffer a setback? Is the potential damage something you could recover from? If you can't recover from the failure, don't do it. For example, if the potential end result of a decision you make means your company misses payroll, even if there's only a small probability of failure, then that's not an acceptable risk because failure would threaten your company. Without appropriately compensated employees, you have no company.

The only possible exception to the "avoid existential risk" mantra is when your business is on the line and you need to make a desperate play to keep going. It's like the end of a close football game, and your team is behind and doesn't have enough time to make it all the way down the field. All you can do is risk losing the game (which you would lose anyway) and throw the ball in a Hail Mary play, hoping somebody on your team will catch it for a touchdown to steal the win.

Only perform that kind of business maneuver when you have excess capability and resources. In that case, you may be able to secure additional worthy business gains, but remember, if your resources are depleted and your choices are null, you're facing a bad situation. A Hail Mary maneuver may be the only choice you have, and it may or may not work. Exercise caution.

GOOD DECISIONS CAN BRING BAD OUTCOMES

You can make a good decision and still get a bad outcome, just as you can make a bad decision and end up with a good outcome. This point is misunderstood by many people. They tend to equate a positive outcome with having made a good decision and a negative outcome with having made a bad decision. They say to themselves, "Since I got a positive outcome, then I must have made a good decision," and the same for the reverse. But that assessment isn't necessarily true.

For example, suppose you go to the casino and bet your house at the gambling table. If it works, people might tell you, "You made a good decision. Now you have two houses!" However, had you lost, they would tell you, "You shouldn't have done that. It was the wrong decision to make." The reality is, if you only have one house, whether you win or lose, it would always be a bad decision to make that bet in the first place.

Outcome doesn't indicate the quality of a decision. I have had people tell me they made a good decision based on the outcome, yet when I look at what they did, the potential for disaster was high, and a failure would have been catastrophic. I don't call that a good decision. Only sound analysis of the circumstances and variables surrounding the decision will tell you whether the decision was good or bad.

People who make decisions based on outcomes may get lucky from time to time, but eventually their luck runs out. Likewise, people might think they've made a bad decision because the outcome wasn't what they expected. But the decision itself, based on a solid risk assessment, was the right one. Either way—good outcome or bad—people who can properly assess risk will stand a better chance of gaining more good outcomes than bad ones.

To apply this concept, classify results of decisions into three categories: (1) inconsequential; (2) somewhat negatively or positively consequential; and (3) significantly negatively or positively consequential. Then drop anything that has an inconsequential potential outcome from your consideration and spend most of your time on the significantly consequential outcomes. Remember to assess the negative consequences in addition to the positive consequences—don't look only at the positive.

MARKETING INFRASTRUCTURE

Your marketing microcompany is responsible for all the processes that drive consumer awareness and knowledge about your product or service. Its main function is to induce your target market to seek more information or declare their interest in making a purchase.

Why is it important to think of marketing as a scalable or sellable unit of your business? Well, companies need to market to continue to thrive and succeed. If there's a problem with the marketing unit, you will see it ripple throughout the entire system. And when something breaks in marketing, that breakage could break down your entire company.

To see marketing as its own company, identify the output of the marketing unit—the product the marketing unit produces. In this case, consumer interest is the product of the marketing unit. You can measure how many people express interest or have engaged with your company. Then you can work backward through all the processes within marketing to fix the problems that are preventing more people from interacting with your company's product. With that information, you'll know where to make improvements that will lead people to express interest in your product.

Improving the design and function of any microcompany to create scalability begins with examining its existing infrastructure. We start with marketing, instead of product or sales, because marketing speaks to your customers, and without customers you don't have a business. The first step is to examine your marketing processes within each marketing channel you've developed and within the overall marketing manufacturing unit. Look at how they work independently and how they are integrated. See each process and channel as part of a larger machine. If one part doesn't work, then fix it or get rid of it. As you build an exit infrastructure, use the following criteria to examine each element of the marketing infrastructure.

MARKETING STAFF

These employees are a key component of your overall marketing infrastructure. Do you have the right marketing staff? Do you have enough marketing staff? Is your marketing staff replaceable? Do you have a marketing staff that is batching procedures, or do they have a uniform, repeatable process that they apply? If one person leaves the company, will a marketing process or channel break down? How would that affect the product?

Your people need the skills to do the job. And you need to organize them so that if anyone leaves, business doesn't come to a screeching halt. All too often, people work at a company for years, master a skill, develop their own processes, and never train anyone else to do it. Worse, they haven't even documented what they do, so there's no guidebook lying around for someone to pick up and learn on the fly. When the resident expert takes a week off, no one knows what to do.

Buyers look at these things. They will ask, "How does the marketing part of your business work?" If you tell them one person does it, they will want to know how it gets done when that person is on vacation. What if that person leaves the company? They will ask these questions because they know that without redundancy in your workforce and a knowledge base to document how tasks are accomplished, you're at high risk of losing productivity.

Your potential buyer is looking for mass production, not craft production. People with unique skills can be considered to be in craft positions. Companies need these people, but they also need documented, replicable systems and processes so they will remain resilient when that craftsperson isn't around. Creating redundancies in terms of your marketing team is a crucial step in providing continuity and scalability in your marketing operations.

SIZE OF MARKET

To scale up your company's architecture and design it to encourage the maximum number of consumers to show interest in your product, you need to understand the size of the market your infrastructure can handle. The size of your market comes with its own limitations, such as consumer acceptance of your product and demand for it. If you're in the business of marketing cattle feed, for example, you will not get millions of interested customers no matter what you do because there's a limited number of cattle ranchers. If you're marketing something like hand sanitizer, on the other hand, your market will be significantly larger. Some of the questions you must ask yourself on a regular basis are: *How big is my market? How much revenue can I pull from that market? Do I need to grow or improve my marketing infrastructure to fully reach my market?* Your answers belong in your marketing plan.

DYNAMIC MARKETING PLANS

Your marketing plan shouldn't be static; it must be scalable and replicable as your ability to attract more customers grows. You must plan, build, and maintain. If you plan to make changes to your product occasionally or regularly, does your infrastructure support those changes? Your business might fluctuate seasonally, like a furniture company that generates a large portion of its revenues from selling dining room sets in the fall while people are thinking about entertaining holiday guests. That same business may switch its focus to patio furniture in the springtime. Can you switch gears and quickly adapt your infrastructure to market the shifting products with minimal disturbance?

In another example, let's say you decided to undertake a TV campaign as part of your marketing. You may have designed your infrastructure to reach a particular community through a particular channel. Is that process replicable in another community, another geographic location, or another market? If so, make this an intentional feature in your planning. And take the view of how this would look when you sell the company. The buyer of your company will want to know the answer to these questions. While they are looking to buy your entire company, the marketing unit affects the viability of their purchase. Their assessment of this microcompany will, to some extent, determine the valuation and the offer they'll make. If you design your marketing infrastructure as an exit infrastructure, it will contribute to a more profitable and self-running overall infrastructure—one that might even make you decide to keep the company even longer.

PLAN B FOR POOR RESULTS

Don't expect all your marketing efforts or plans to work out as expected just because you think you've accounted for every contingency. Maybe your target demographics changed over time, for example, skewing your perspective. No matter how well you plan, you can only predict the results to a degree. Plan A will sometimes fail.

Even a plan that works well one time—or hundreds of times—isn't guaranteed to work every time. When your company relies on marketing efforts to generate revenues, any unexpected change can create a revenue problem. Be prepared with a Plan B.

Consider the following scenario. You have a $100,000 marketing budget. There are a number of ways you might use that budget. In this scenario, you decide to spend it all on one campaign. Maybe it's a short campaign, and you feel comfortable with it. You feel safe making the projections; odds are you're going to be able to recoup all costs and make a profit. Sounds good.

But if the campaign fails and you've invested all of your marketing dollars, then you'll end up losing it all. You'll have a hard time starting again. Depending on good luck isn't a substitute for sound business practices.

You should always have a Plan B, a fallback position that will help you recover if your Plan A doesn't work out. Your buyer will be looking for a marketing disaster recovery plan that would preserve the value of your company in the case of a failure. If your marketing infrastructure and planning aren't designed from that perspective, your buyer will consider all that could go wrong and will be likely to offer less for your company.

As with other elements of an exit infrastructure, what works for the buyer works for you as the owner. If you have all of this set up in the right way (including contingency planning) and create a steady stream of revenues for your company, you earn more profit. And reaping those rewards will allow you to spend more of your capital on improving more of your infrastructure for more time and freedom. It's a virtuous cycle.

Marketing is a critical microcompany within your business that needs careful inspection and solid strategy—a well-made infrastructure. But it's only one example. The other parts of your company demand the same if you want a business-wide exit infrastructure that produces stellar results and attracts potential buyers.

OUTLIVE YOUR COMPETITORS

Business owners with an Exit Mindset extend the concept of Plan B far beyond the marketing arena. Remember that a buyer looking at your company will not be thinking only about your company. They will also be thinking about what will happen to your business if some other company introduces a competitive product to the market. How will you maintain your marketing footprint? Is your infrastructure set up to accommodate that? Or, more importantly, to respond to that?

You need to be ready to respond, and quickly, as Intel did in the late 1970s, when Motorola introduced its own chip that could have created an existential threat to Intel. It might have eliminated Intel's advantage entirely. Within three months, though, Intel had modified their existing chip and reconfigured their operations to keep them in front. How did they do it? Intel had an existing chip model design in their infrastructure for addressing competitive threats. All they had to do was execute. Regardless of the size of your company, you always need to have procedures ready to go to address competitive threats.

SALES INFRASTRUCTURE

Many business owners confuse marketing and sales, which results in their inability to create a scalable business, which in turn makes it difficult to structure an optimal exit. If you don't understand the distinction between marketing and sales, you tend to be inefficient in both. If you do understand, you'll build a company that has a good marketing infrastructure followed by a scalable sales infrastructure, a company that commands a better purchase price and enjoys a stronger revenue stream.

Marketing comprises advertising and other activities that first get people's attention and pull them into a conversation with you. Once the consumer starts interacting, the sales process begins. Sales infrastructure is everything that happens from the expression of initial interest through to the completed transaction—it includes things like communication from your sales team and product demonstrations. Your sales infrastructure supports everything that happens within this process.

Your sales infrastructure's job is to create a monetary transaction in exchange for the product offered. Depending on the business, the line between marketing and sales may be blurred or transparent to the consumer. No approach is necessarily good or bad, as there are many very successful products that require their own specific approaches to marketing and sales. You might have a business that sells products solely online, so you combine marketing and sales within a single automated workflow. On your website, customers can see a product and a price, read a product description and reviews, and buy the product all in one stop. That's great for you, but it won't be the best choice for every business. The key is to find the approach that fits your business model best, and is scalable and replicable.

SALES STAFF

In your sales infrastructure, you might discover a dependency on specific people who would be difficult, if not impossible, to replace. If there's no infrastructure in place for hiring, training, and getting a new salesperson up to speed quickly, sales will be lost.

The reason? Salespeople have capacity limits. For example, if you have twenty salespeople, no matter how skilled they are, they can only commit so much time to selling. Companies have capacity limits, too—the number of products they can turn out. If a company's sales force can't serve the company's capacity needs, there's a problem with the infrastructure. It's likely that the company will need to hire more salespeople and/or improve the sales infrastructure (by adding more sales support staff, for example) to allow people to sell more products.

Not having a robust sales infrastructure will also put your exit plan at risk. Just like with your marketing staff, a failure in your ability to find, train, and replace sales staff means your company's buyer will either lose interest or they will offer you a lower price than you want. In this scenario, a savvy buyer will look at your capacity and know you don't have enough salespeople. They'll see you don't have a process for replacing people who leave. Some buyers are skilled at bringing in new people and getting them trained quickly, and they see how they could dramatically increase revenue with that infrastructure fix. But that takes work—work they will have to do. They may pay you slightly more based on the potential in your infrastructure, but they'll pay much more if you have an infrastructure that's built with an Exit Mindset already in place.

SALES PROCESSES

Processes—including sales processes—that are easily and seamlessly repeatable will bring the biggest payoff when you exit your company. I encourage you to build easily repeatable processes into your sales infrastructure to make it scalable; you'll find this beneficial when your market grows, or when your company's product capacity grows.

Keep in mind the importance of having the different pieces of your company architecture work well together. The processes of individual departments must be coordinated. Lack of coordination between management and the sales unit is a common stumbling block here. In my experience, the management of many companies misses the fact that training and support systems are key components of sales infrastructures. Most of those systems and processes are deployed ad hoc, without a formalized strategy. If you or your managers have to acquire talent and train differently every single time, then your sales infrastructure isn't scalable, and it doesn't conform to an exit infrastructure.

Having a well-conceived sales process is important, but there has to be a balance between having a rigid process that ensures predictability and scalability and being so rigid that you fail to capitalize on your core talents and capabilities within that sales infrastructure. Err on the side of consistency. That's how you create an infrastructure that allows you to lower risk, improve predictability, scale as needed, and eventually enjoy more time and higher income for yourself.

PRODUCT DELIVERY INFRASTRUCTURE

Processes within the product delivery infrastructure should be well organized, precise, carefully thought out, scalable, and capable of handling common mishaps in the delivery process. Your ultimate goal is to create a system that allows your products to get to the consumer without late, non-delivery, or wrong product issues.

There are more things to consider when it comes to a delivery process beyond the transportation of product to the customer. Other issues involve logistics, packaging, and communication with the end user. Then there are the unanticipated problems. If you look at the amount of thinking that some of the large corporations put into the delivery process, you will realize that if you want to scale up, you'll need to adopt some of those same systems into your own company.

Let's consider a simple example. Say you're a furniture manufacturer. Your latest marketing campaign was a greater success than predicted and brought many people into your showroom. Your salespeople closed many deals. Everything's looking great until you realize that you don't have enough delivery trucks to get all that product to the customers. Your infrastructure can't accommodate more product without disrupting your operation. Now what? Delivery infrastructure has to be considered any time you increase capacity at a company or do something that increases demand or sales. If it isn't, excess sales will likely create issues that can impact delivery and customer satisfaction.

If you think that the example above doesn't apply to you because you're a service-based business, think again. Let's consider another example. If a law firm takes on more clients than it can handle, the company won't be able to deliver legal services on time. The owners can take on the additional clients and fail, or they can turn down the new clients and lose the opportunity to generate more revenues. From an Exit Mindset perspective, if a buyer wants to pay for the law firm, then they will value it as nothing but a small, non-scalable enterprise, and they will offer a correspondingly reduced price for it. A smart buyer wants to know how you handle increases in capacity and other events that demand full use of your delivery process and the infrastructure that supports it. If you don't have an answer, the buyer will adjust the price.

Exit Mindset companies plan for changes in demand as a matter of routine. If you're a midsize or large company, don't wait until a change in demand becomes an issue that ends up creating a big problem for you. You'll lose revenues, and you may lose customers; you'll certainly lose credibility around your ability to manage product delivery. You simply can't scale a business with an infrastructure that doesn't allow for changes in product demand.

PRODUCT SUPPORT INFRASTRUCTURE

Nordstrom, the department store, has always viewed strong customer service as a promotable, marketable customer benefit. One of their customer interactions became the stuff of legend and a case study for business schools around the country, and it remains relevant.

Nordstrom's mantra was to make getting refunds easy for customers: "We take everything back without question or reason." The story goes (and it was confirmed) that a customer once returned a set of four winter tires he bought from a store that Nordstrom had previously acquired. That store sold linens and various clothing items, in addition to tires. The associate in charge of the return promptly made a discreet inquiry and then gave the customer a refund for his purchase in cash.

Nordstrom itself has never sold tires, but the employee, knowing the company's policy, wanted the customer to be satisfied. Obviously, Nordstrom absorbed the loss and the inventory, but it won the hearts of customers nationwide.

Just as product delivery infrastructures are separate infrastructure units, so too is product support (sometimes called customer support or customer experience). Your marketing, product development, and sales teams have done their part to acquire the customer, so you already have an investment in the customer, and they liked your product enough to buy it. After all that work, you don't want your product support people to fumble the ball at the goal line.

This infrastructure unit is important for one simple reason: It's easier to sell to an existing customer than to a new customer. That's why companies with existing, happy, repeat customers are much more highly valued than those constantly struggling to acquire new customers. And also why you should never ignore the lifetime value of a customer.

When I decide to buy a company, I am usually looking at the customer acquisition cost. I want it to be reasonable, but I'm also looking at other factors, such as customer loyalty and lifetime value. When you develop these things to your advantage, it's natural you'll reap some of the rewards immediately in terms of profits and time saved while running your business. But you also stand to gain (or lose) valuation when your company is being bought. You won't get a great valuation if you're constantly seeking to acquire new customers. This makes product support extremely important.

The quickest way to lose a customer is through bad postsale support. You have to build your exit customer support infrastructure methodically and carefully. This is the first thing to ask yourself: *Does our support infrastructure have what it takes to support our customers? Does it have breaking points? If so, are they self-healing, or do they require massive intervention?* (Self-healing means that a breakdown can be fixed internally without major intervention or loss of productivity.) *Is there a clear-cut infrastructure for that?* If the answer to any of these questions is no, now is the time to address it.

Let me give you an example. Say part of your support infrastructure is phone lines. You have fifty people available to answer incoming customer calls. What happens if you sell more products than usual in one month and those calls increase by 30 percent? Or if there's a problem with a product and you receive many additional inquiries and requests? Do you have the infrastructure to support all those people and the calls? Do you have a process that would remedy the situation effectively and quickly? A remedy can take many forms. You might establish a process for giving customer support staff more hours during unexpected busy times. Perhaps you can create a process for quickly hiring more people to answer the phones. Another option could be to outsource your overflow calls to another company that specializes in support calls. You could ask an outsource center to take the call and enter the customer's information into your database so you can reach out to them later instead of putting someone on hold for fifteen minutes. There could be many solutions.

To be adequately prepared, your product support infrastructure must be set up for these possibilities well in advance. You want to plan for these kinds of contingencies ahead of time, before a problem occurs, so you can respond quickly when it does.

The issue of customer support infrastructure isn't trivial. Many companies have folded or been damaged by this problem. They were overwhelmed because they either sold too many products too quickly or sold a product that had problems they weren't equipped to support. This not only hurts the business's reputation but can turn into a public relations and financial nightmare. Not all who experience this kind of disaster recover.

RESEARCH AND DEVELOPMENT INFRASTRUCTURE

Many people associate research and development with high tech or large companies. The fact is, if you're in any kind of business, you already have some form of an R&D department.

You may not think of it as an R&D department, but I can assure you it exists. Every time you think of an improvement in what you do, you're conducting R&D. Every time someone in your company comes to you with ideas and suggestions about how to improve your product, you're doing R&D. It may have occurred organically and without a formalized process, but that doesn't make it any less important.

Once you grasp that fact, you can evolve from having occasional "I have an idea" events into developing a formal process that allows scalability and creates a better exit infrastructure, which you can leverage in your negotiations with the buyer of your company. Not to mention you accrue increased benefits from the revenues you generate with improved products and new product lines. Be intentional about making research and development part of your infrastructure. Even if your R&D department is just one person, always be thinking about what you can learn from their work and how you can use that knowledge to make a better product.

Research and development is very often a company's most underfunded and overlooked infrastructure component. People tend to be myopic about product improvement; they can't see the need to continuously improve their offerings. However, some companies are very methodical about gathering and caring for ideas. They do trial after trial before launching an improved version of a product or a whole new product to replace one they're retiring.

You must do the same to attain an Exit Mindset. Methodical improvement of your product, as a matter of course, is imperative, particularly if your industry is competitive and rapidly evolving. No buyer will show interest in a company whose product has a short lifecycle. They want to know you have the systems, mechanisms, and infrastructure to continuously improve the offering. A strong R&D infrastructure also increases customer satisfaction and helps ensure customer retention, leading to even more profits for you and less time spent acquiring each new customer.

You can and should apply R&D strategies across the board to products, marketing, sales methods, product delivery, and customer support. That's how great products develop—they don't just start out that way. Always question whether there's a better way. Avoid the status quo, or be left behind.

RELATIONSHIPS ARE PART OF YOUR INFRASTRUCTURE

Most people associate infrastructure with physical objects and work-related processes and systems. But few of them put corporate and business relationships in that category. These are different from personal relationships. While there's no doubt that an element of personal relationships exists within the boundaries of business and corporate relations, the primary driver of those relationships is usually business interests on both sides. This means that regardless of your personal relationship with the people involved, they care more about your business with them, and you care more about their business with you. The business transaction is simply that—a transaction. The clarity here is actually a great thing—it creates common ground between companies and people to achieve a desired objective that's beneficial for everyone from a business perspective.

Fostering business relationships allows you to build bridges between your business and others. This is important because once you establish common ground between business relationships, it will be easier for you to develop a good relationship infrastructure.

A good relationship infrastructure consists of a set of relationships that are built on continuity and mutual benefit. Boundaries are established, and procedures are clearly defined. Having such a relationship infrastructure will help your company grow and expand and establish skill sets and capabilities that you wouldn't necessarily have without working with others.

Once you've developed a good number of relationships that enhance and improve your leverage and are based on business instead of personal interest, you will have built a key part of your exit infrastructure. When you sell the company and leave it, the buyer will reap the benefit of those existing relationships without you. That has lasting value.

Look for opportunities to build relationships everywhere. You might partner with product or parts manufacturers and vendors or form strategic alliances. Too many business owners don't leverage these relationships, even though doing so would push them to optimal growth and scale. For example, the choice between two suppliers could impact the scalability of your business. So always be on the lookout for companies that complement your processes. In addition, too many owners don't understand that each of their relationships has the potential to make a difference in the overall infrastructure of their company. Choose the right ones and you're in for a nice growth spurt!

Let's say you're in the business of meatless products. Building a relationship infrastructure might mean you would look for a vendor that provides packaging that keeps the product fresher longer. That business relationship, just one of many you have, can create a significant addition to your revenues through additional sales and good will. You'd be surprised; it might even cut your costs. Now you're scoring on two fronts!

Look for companies that do one thing well on a large scale that can take over part of your process at a lower cost and do a better job so you can deliver a better product. The company might specialize in marketing, sales, or delivery. It might be able to create a better website. Something that simple—done well—could have a massive impact on your company.

Try to identify those vendor relationships that improve your product or infrastructure and allow you to scale. That may mean making some changes in who you work with. I am sure you have certain vendor relationships you're satisfied with. But if those relationships don't work to your advantage, then consider switching to someone new. After all, you have a duty to yourself and your employees to build the best infrastructure possible, and you owe it to yourself to have a business that can command the highest valuation when you decide to cash it out.

How important are business and corporate relationships? It's absolutely the case that having even a single productive corporate relationship could translate into a meaningful impact on company valuation. A buyer places a higher value on a company with existing relationships that are strong, credible, and beneficial to both sides than one that doesn't. They also see your relationships as evidence that your business is one that can scale; it has the necessary partnerships in place with other people and companies to rely on, whether or not you, the business owner, are around.

MANAGEMENT INFRASTRUCTURE

There's one last piece to the infrastructure puzzle that you must not overlook: your company's management infrastructure. Quality executives and managers are crucial ingredients for success. As the owner of your company, you probably already spend a great deal of time working with your management team, assessing their capabilities, and trying to position them for success so they can help the company grow. Now you need to make them shine even more.

Potential buyers of your company are going to take a sharp look at the individuals comprising your management team. And more than likely they'll want to interview them. I've seen promising deals fall apart at the last moment when the buyer wasn't confident that a company's management team was going to be able to implement planned new initiatives and changes.

Make an objective assessment of your management staff. Does the all-important sales department have a competent leader who consistently produces strong results? Is the product development team well led, always keeping their eyes focused on product refinement and meeting customers' wants and needs? What about the management team in charge of your company's infrastructure? Do the production and delivery units run smoothly? What about customer support?

A prudent buyer will seek answers to all of these questions, so it's in your interests to have the best management team you can find in place before selling your company. Each element of your functioning infrastructure, including management, must be operating at an optimal level in order to garner your company the valuation it deserves.

CHAPTER 9 *EXERCISE*

Key questions for developing your company's exit infrastructure:

Are funds appropriately allocated within your business? If not, what changes will you implement?

Are your departmental budgets distinct and detailed? If not, how will you improve them?

Which elements of your infrastructure depend on personnel versus being self-sufficient?

Do you have irreplaceably skilled individuals in your company? If so, how can you mitigate this risk?

How would a process breakdown impact your product/output? What are your contingency plans?

Are your major systems and processes documented? If not, how will you address this?

What is the size of your market? Is it growing or shrinking?

Do you have an R&D process for quick market adaptation? If not, what is your plan?

Can you swiftly scale output in response to market changes? If not, how will you enhance this capacity?

Can your product support staff manage a rapid increase in output? If not, what is your strategy?

Does your management team add value in the eyes of potential buyers? If not, what improvements can be made?

STRATEGIES FOR CLARIFYING INFRASTRUCTURE PROBLEMS

HAVE YOU EVER CONFRONTED A PROBLEM AND wondered where to begin? I certainly have. Over the years, I have adopted a number of strategies and tactics to break that deadlock. I will mention some of the important ones here. Remember, these are strategies to help you along the road, and you can modify them to suit your own unique situation. Obviously, building the right company infrastructure will occupy a good portion of your time. No one can predict all the things you will need to work on, but I've given you some food for thought in this chapter in the hope that I'll stimulate your thinking on the subject. Use these strategies as platforms to launch your thinking into the problem-solving possibilities that exist in your own situation.

CLARIFYING THE PROBLEM IS 90 PERCENT OF THE SOLUTION

Too often, business owners facing a problem jump on a solution right away without actually knowing what the problem is. That's the exact opposite of what you should do. Most of the time that you spend addressing a problem should be spent figuring out and understanding what the problem is. Once you have a detailed understanding of the problem, you'll have plenty of time to find the solution, and that solution will be much easier to implement. I've seen many people get to the wrong solution or spend enormous amounts of time they didn't need to spend, simply because they weren't clear about what the problem was.

The best way to assess a problem situation is to first identify how you want the particular infrastructure to perform and break that result into its various components. Then do an analytical deep dive into the issues that could come into play with each component. Are these issues in marketing, sales, product delivery, or product support? Where are the bottlenecks? Look at the people working within those functions, too. Are they weak points? Are they replaceable? If the people are solid, are they perhaps receiving insufficient resources? Answering these questions will help you find a solution that's permanent, scalable, and resilient.

It's not always easy to see the infrastructure components clearly when you're intimately involved in the business. And there's no one way to approach a problem analysis, because every business is different, with different infrastructures, processes, and people. You have to put some serious thought into discovering where you are and what you want to achieve, and then be proactive about making the changes needed to get there.

VISUALIZE THE ISSUES INVOLVED

Create a high-level view of the problem-solving process so you don't get caught up in the details and lose sight of what you're trying to accomplish. As mentioned, you first want to clarify the major infrastructure functions and components and then isolate the components that you want to improve or replace. This should help clarify infrastructure priorities. Keep your focus on working on the actual processes and structures needed to accomplish the best exit infrastructure you can develop, and remember to look at the people, processes, and management around the function you designed. Always ask yourself if they could be designed differently to better support your exit infrastructure.

Adapting your infrastructure requires flexible thinking on your part. Anything goes during this imagine phase. There are no obstacles. Think openly and don't get hung up on what you believe isn't possible. Instead of focusing on what you can't do or can't control, focus on what you want to achieve and the end result.

TRY MIND MAPPING

Sometimes, it can be difficult to visualize the different parts of your infrastructure in your mind, so putting it on paper, a white board, or in digital form helps you see the whole picture. Mind maps—graphical representations of the infrastructure unit you're working on—are one of the best tools to help you break down the problem so you can see what you really have. They excel at showing the relationships and hierarchies between different components. Making a mind map will help you clarify your thinking. It will also help you to communicate what you're thinking to others.

DON'T FORGET RESOURCE MANAGEMENT

Wisely managing your company's resources is probably the single most important thing you must learn to do well when developing an exit strategy. No company has unlimited resources to immediately and simultaneously fix all of its problems and create a dream infrastructure. Even some of the most valued companies in the world can't afford to do everything they want.

You have to allocate your time and company money to the right infrastructure units until you get close to what you want. To do this, you must determine the resources you need for your desired outcomes—what to do, who will do it, and how much it will cost. Then prioritize deployment based on resource availability. Next, prioritize where you want to put your time and resources—your finances and your people—for maximum yield.

Focus on big objectives. Think long-term. For example, an improvement to your sales infrastructure that produces only a temporary bump in sales isn't necessarily a good use of your resources if you can achieve superior results by using those resources to create a long-term solution and a scalable sales infrastructure. It's more beneficial to deploy your resources in a manner that can create a more stable stream of sales for the next five years with a system or a model that's self-running, scalable, and replicable.

Setting priorities is key when developing product delivery infrastructure, as it is when building all of the exit structures you need to entice potential buyers to your company (and reap the rewards while you wait for one to come). Decide which units will deliver the highest yield and you will increase the value of the deliverable and the company itself if you dedicate resources to them. Look at the big picture, determine what will have the greatest impact, and allocate your resources accordingly. Once you have a strategy for transforming your infrastructure into an exit infrastructure, continually evaluate that plan to make sure you're effectively deploying it. Constantly check the deployed infrastructure against the stated infrastructure strategy.

Decide who will be in charge of deployment for each infrastructure unit. Give unit leaders the directive of building an architecture that achieves the goal of boosting the overall performance of the company, not providing temporary fixes. This is a tough lesson for many entrepreneurs. You must learn to let go and give other people leadership responsibilities and accountability.

Delegating responsibility is necessary, and doable, even in a small company. Let's say you have four people working for you; perhaps you can assign each one a leadership role, even if they aren't fully qualified for that role. If they're the right people, they will learn and adapt, and of course you can mentor them. By taking this step, you create a dynamic that facilitates the process of adding more people, who in turn you can develop to take on more responsibilities.

This is where you start developing leaders and leadership skills for the team. Believe me, you'll need them. But it's important to make sure everyone on the team understands the mission—which is to create an infrastructure that's scalable and sustainable. Make that clear. Make an organizational chart with names, functions, and responsibilities, if it helps.

TAKE A TOP-DOWN VERSUS BOTTOM-UP APPROACH

When trying to solve infrastructure problems, avoid what most people do, which is to focus on localized problems. Typically, those visible problems, while not the biggest ones, are the loudest and most prominent. The bigger problems are usually quiet and less evident. Yet, if you don't address the big problems, you end up with a continuous stream of issues that never ends.

I call localized problems "by-product problems"; they are offshoots from the root cause. When you don't address the root cause, those by-product problems will consume much of your time. However, by taking a top-down approach when looking at your infrastructure, you'll gain needed perspective, and be able to identify the big-picture problem that's creating the little problems. This will create the biggest leverage within your Exit Mindset. What that means is you have to be a high-level strategic thinker when you're looking at your infrastructure, and then drill down to the tactical issues that need to be addressed. Don't get bogged down by the small details when you need to be looking at the big picture.

USE A SELF-LOCKING MECHANISM

An exit strategy infrastructure demands a "self-locking mechanism." By that I mean a procedure, within a system, that lessens the possibility of a mistake or triggers an alarm if the system doesn't operate appropriately. Think of it as a tripwire designed to alert you when something is going wrong. Having such a procedure in place is useful because it's not always immediately obvious when a mistake is made. A tripwire alerts management to the problem. The more tripwires you have in your infrastructure, the more security you build, because they allow your company to spot errors as they occur so they don't go undetected and worsen.

I use self-locking mechanisms a lot in developing systems and procedures for my companies. For example, let's say your sales department sells an item and receives payment only upon delivery. A self-locking mechanism here might be having your sales report go to both the sales manager and your accounting department. You would be able to catch any delivery issue through your accounting department, because they would track the number of payments they received. If that number doesn't match up with the number of sales reported, then there could be a delivery issue. Being alerted to that possibility would allow you to investigate how your delivery cycles are working.

You can calibrate the sensitivity of your tripwire to suit your needs. If your metric is 100 percent delivery in two days, for example, and your customer service is getting one "late arrival" delivery a week, this might not be a cause to act. If you get one alarm per day, however, you'll want to scrutinize each part of the delivery system, from order taking to the truck at the customer's door, to make sure you locate the problem and fix it—and then watch it carefully. Of course, your customer service reports will let you know if there's a subsequent recurrence weeks or months later.

Tripwire monitoring can be relatively simple. It could be as easy as assigning a person to periodically check a certain metric. The simple action of checking would generate an alert if something had gone wrong in a process.

The best self-locking mechanisms hinge on an automated action. Most alert mechanisms depend on management and reports, but those approaches are often too error prone because people can be too distracted with other work to spot a potential problem. There's no such thing as a 100 percent fail-safe system, but by building automated tripwires into your infrastructure design, a small problem is less likely to become a much bigger one.

CHAPTER 10 *EXERCISE*

Reflect on the following while evaluating your infrastructure:

? What is the most pressing infrastructure issue currently impacting my business, and how could resolving it significantly drive progress?

After identifying the critical infrastructure issue, place it at the center of a blank page. Create a mindmap branching into three key aspects of this problem. For each of these aspects, brainstorm three potential solutions utilizing the techniques discussed in this chapter.

Replicate this procedure for two additional infrastructure issues you are facing. Practice this exercise bi-monthly.

MINDMAP

Infrastructure Problem

CHAPTER 11

GETTING YOUR INFRASTRUCTURE TO GREAT

NOW IT'S TIME TO FOCUS ON THE BIG PICTURE and discuss the things you need to do to take your infrastructure to the next level and increase its appeal to buyers. In this chapter, we will discuss several tools to help you do just that, including stress testing your company to make sure its various parts work well together, using key performance indicators to monitor your various units, and getting accustomed to performing objective evaluations of your company.

ESTABLISH CONNECTION

In most of Part Three of this book, we have been talking about improving, modifying, or replacing individual infrastructure units. Even though you're looking at these units as stand-alone internal microcompanies, you must also examine how well they work together so that you can ensure processes move seamlessly from one part of the company to the next. A seamless hand-off between infrastructure units ensures that your company's workflow runs without interruption. This means appropriate systems need to be set up to establish connections between your different units. These connections could involve a combination of software, machines, and people.

For instance, some businesses connect their infrastructure units by using just-in-time (JIT) production to seamlessly create outputs at the exact same time as the next process requires them. An example of JIT is the point-of-sale scanner system at a grocery store, which logs when an item is sold and informs an employee when the item needs to be restocked so it's ready for the next customer. This is efficient, and there's less chance of running out of items, which leads to shortages and lost sales.

Communication between people within each unit is also consequential. A well-known example of disconnected communication is the US government intelligence apparatus prior to 9/11. Many of the government intelligence agencies responsible for detecting the potential threat had bits and pieces of information but did not communicate that information to other governmental agencies. Therefore, the flow of information was not effective, creating a missed opportunity to detect the threat before that dreadful attack. If you compare this to the lack of connection between various infrastructure units in your company, I imagine you can see the parallels. In the government's case, they responded with an overhaul, creating the Department of Homeland Security, which oversees the various intelligence-gathering agencies and coordinates the information they produce. Do you think your business should be treated as seriously?

Amazon is another example of an organization that works

hard on seamless workflow among its business units. A customer places an order online, and it's transmitted to a fulfillment center where it's picked, packed, and shipped. Sounds simple enough. Yet, even with robots and computers, the selected merchandise has to be picked from items supplied by one of a few hundred thousand vendors. Sometimes this process is handled by third-party vendors who receive orders directly from Amazon to be shipped directly to customers. Sometimes, the order fulfillment process occurs through third-party vendors who keep their inventory in Amazon's warehouses; in this case, the order is shipped by Amazon but restocked by the vendor based on the numbers. And of course sometimes the fulfillment process occurs as a purchase by Amazon from the vendor, and sold by Amazon to the retail customer; Amazon then reorders the item using a program that anticipates future ordering from vendors. Additionally, some orders are for products manufactured, published, or created by Amazon itself directly for sale. Amazon takes all these points of communication seriously in order for the customer's package to reliably reach their door. And finally, in a related example of infrastructure connectivity, some of Amazon's marketing units scan the entire product line available through the Amazon website—hundreds of thousands of products—for strong-selling products that Amazon could consider private labeling.

Unfortunately, lack of communication among different business units is all too common. You must create seamless integration among all of your company's units. You must ensure that your company's units communicate and coordinate to produce better information flow and to encourage collaborative outcomes. Without this connectivity, your business is less efficient, and revenue and value suffer. Your exit infrastructure will not be so desirable to a buyer unless you have connectivity.

Again, back up and take a high-level view. You can isolate each unit, whether R&D, customer support, marketing, etc., to create amazing, scalable segments, but your higher perspective is needed to make sure they all work together to create a true exit infrastructure, one that will get you a higher valuation for your company. But here again, the benefits of this transcend beyond valuation. Create connected infrastructure and you'll create a scalable, profitable model that gives you time to do the things you want to do, including making your exit or not exiting at all.

ASSIGN KEY PERFORMANCE INDICATORS TO EACH INFRASTRUCTURE UNIT

Key performance indicators (KPIs) inform you about those actions that make the biggest difference, bring the highest yield, and move the company furthest in the right direction. Too many businesses don't use key performance indicators. Instead, they collect numbers from all over, and with too many numbers to analyze, paralysis sets in. In my experience, they would be better off using KPIs to identify the most important numbers or indicators. The benefit of being selective about your KPIs is that you can keep your focus.

You could see this concept in practice if you ever visited an airplane cockpit. You would notice the massive amounts of indicators and instrumentation on the dashboard, of course, but do you really think the pilots are watching each one of them throughout the entire flight? Of course not! They are only focused on a few key indicators, but can use the others as needed. Think of yourself as a pilot. Pilots don't stare at the controls when flying. If all they did was watch the gauges, they'd have no time to fly the plane.

Analysis paralysis, caused when too much data enters the decision-making process, can be a real problem. In one of my companies, we filled screens and screens with every metric you can imagine. We needed those screens to accommodate the massive amounts of spreadsheets we were looking at and analyzing. It didn't take too long to realize this approach was diluting our focus. The information was so granular it was hard to get a real sense of the important KPIs. So, we ended up eliminating the screens in favor of basic KPIs with drilled-down data behind them. That allowed us to take action and set strategy.

So how do you decide which metrics are your KPIs? When it comes to your exit infrastructure, every unit should have one particular KPI you can look at to decide whether the unit needs attention. If it does, then dig deeper. For example, when you're looking at your sales team's performance—look at your sales revenue or the number of units sold. Don't get mired in worrying about who you sold to, or the demographic, or how many of each unit a consumer purchased. That's all good information, but paying attention to every available piece of data could water down your ability to focus on strategies and methods to increase sales, which are the most important things from a business owner or CEO perspective.

When you focus on KPIs and work toward resolving the problems of those that don't meet your measure for success, you might be surprised how often the details beneath the KPIs take care of themselves. I'm not suggesting at all you disregard any underlying problems just because the top line looks good. Just don't lose sight of the important KPIs.

Ultimately, one of the most effective ways to ensure your company is self-running is to put in place a properly structured KPI system. Any potential buyer of the company will also look at those KPIs and their history and decide if your company is worth what you're asking for it. But the intent to sell your company aside, taking this approach will give you even more profits and time.

STRESS TEST YOUR EXIT INFRASTRUCTURE

One of the best ways to demonstrate the value of your company is to show it will withstand various adverse conditions. No one can prepare for everything, of course, but if you're aware of potentially problematic scenarios and you do at least some minor preparation, then you will be ready and able to react quickly should problems arise.

To test your readiness, create various stress test scenarios based on your business, industry, and situation. Surprises are the worst thing that can happen to your infrastructure, so avoid them by inventing worst-case scenarios and figuring out how your infrastructure would handle them. In my companies, I have developed infrastructures to accommodate work outside the office. To me, it was a simple usage of technology to prepare for any unexpected eventuality, not to mention it was helpful to the company. When the coronavirus pandemic struck, many companies were caught off-guard because they didn't have a plan for working from home. They lost productivity while they were figuring out what kind of hardware, software, and networking their people needed to continue working.

One of my friends, who is the CEO of one of the largest companies in the US, told me that prior to 2007, they stress tested their company against several major events. First, they wanted to see what would happen to their company if a few European countries' economies collapsed. Second, they tested against a scenario where the US goes to war with various adversaries. The third test simulated a total collapse of the US financial market.

Most of the executives at the company thought the third scenario was too far-fetched. After all, a collapse of the real estate market the size of the one in 2007 was not very plausible at the time. They figured that it wasn't worth their time to consider, but they decided to assign a small 3 percent probability to it. In an attempt to cover their bases, they tested it anyway and devised a strategy for dealing with it, should it ever occur. When the real estate markets collapsed in 2007, they were one of the few companies that had a plan, which they immediately pulled off the shelf and put into action. They were prepared, and not only did they survive, but they also had the resources to acquire other companies that were falling apart.

Putting your company's infrastructure through stress tests will show you where your company's weak points are so you can strengthen them while times are good. It will help you sleep better at night, too, knowing that your business and your people are prepared to deal with the unexpected. These situations may never happen, but if they do, you'll survive, and possibly even prosper, as my friend's company did. The buyer of your company will also put a higher valuation on it when they see that you have backup plans for unexpected eventualities.

TAKE SOME TIME OFF

This isn't what it sounds like. Of course, I want you to take time off. In fact, part of this book is meant to help you have the availability to take time off. But what I am talking about here is testing your infrastructure's durability and stability by stepping away for various time periods to see if the company can run without you. But watch from a distance. If there's trouble, you can step in.

Can you imagine if you stepped away for a couple of months

and your company kept running smoothly? Better yet, maybe even improved? If that happens, great. But if instead you see massive problems occurring because you aren't there, then you have a problem to solve. Identify the defective infrastructures—perhaps it's the financial unit, or maybe marketing—that rely on your being there. Fix them and leave again. See what happens this time.

I'm not suggesting you do this without a careful and methodical approach. But if you keep doing it over and over again, you'll get to a point where your company runs without you. When that happens, the Exit Mindset will have paid off, and you will have achieved freedom and profits and command a higher valuation.

DO YOUR OWN OBJECTIVE VALUATION

In Part Two, I discussed valuation in terms of building an exit product. Here, I want to talk about another form of "stepping back" where you undertake an objective valuation of your business. A valuation you do yourself will of course be colored by your feelings about your business. If you started the business or you've been running it for a long time, you'll be emotionally attached. But you can't let your emotions affect your calculation of the actual value. Potential buyers won't care how much you love your company. They want to know its actual worth. Take the emotion out of the equation and ask: *What would a buyer pay for my company? What would I pay for it if I were a buyer? Could I sell my company in its current state? What would I get for it?*

This objective valuation process will tell you a lot about your business. It will tell you its selling points, but will also reveal its weaknesses and show you missed opportunities. You might discover that everything is fine and there are no weaknesses, but also find that you have assets you haven't optimized, or monetized, or taken full advantage of. Those missed opportunities are going to keep your valuation lower than it could be.

If it's too hard to get the emotional distance needed for this exercise, in most industries you can hire someone to do an outside valuation. Get an expert analysis of your company's worth in the current market. Ask why it's valued at a certain price and why it's higher or lower than you expected.

GETTING THE VALUATION YOU WANT

I'm a big believer in reverse-engineering what you want to accomplish. In other words, look at your target, decide you're going to achieve it, and only then decide how. To gain an Exit Mindset, you must decide on the number you want from the buyer of your company. Not the number that everybody else thinks you should have, or the number that you currently have, but the number *you* want. Once you decide on that number, don't let anyone convince you otherwise. Once you know where you want to go, start working toward it.

I am convinced this is where your best innovations will come from. Why? Because when you make a decision to go after something, you start doing two things. The first is to think about the target, and the second is to take action. Combining those with persistence creates results. The operative word here is *persistence*, because you'll have some successes and some failures along this journey.

How to reverse engineer your selling number? Review Chapters 1 and 2 on how to value your company and note the ideas on increasing your valuation. Put it all together and come up with a target selling valuation for your company. Now you know what to aim for!

CHAPTER 11 *EXERCISE*

To ensure optimal coordination among various aspects of your infrastructure, consider the following questions:

How effectively do various departments in your company interact? If not well, what measures can you take to improve this?

What steps can you take to encourage robust inter-departmental communication?

Have you identified key performance indicators (KPIs) for every unit? If yes, has this clarified decision-making? If not, what is your plan to define them?

Are you avoiding analysis paralysis by limiting tracked metrics? If not, what is your strategy to streamline metric tracking?

Have you conducted a stress test on your company? If not, what is holding you back, and what insights could you potentially gain post stress test?

Have you thought of spending time away from your business for a detached assessment of strengths and weaknesses?

How can you reverse-engineer your desired company valuation to gauge its feasibility? Upon this analysis, which areas need enhancement to increase your valuation?

PART FOUR

EXIT CONVERSATIONS

DEFINING THE EXIT CONVERSATION

A COMMON DEFINITION OF A CONVERSATION IS "a dialogue between two or more people." In this book, and in the Exit Mindset, the conversation is more expansive. The **exit conversation** is a deliberate and systemized process of engaging the consumer's consciousness and unconsciousness through verbal and nonverbal dialogue. This dialogue creates impressions, appeal, congruency, and demand for your product; ultimately, it creates a connection between you and your target demographics. It also helps you create a scalable and repeatable system for developing and maintaining favorable relationships with your customers and the public in the future. The ultimate intention is to create a long-term positioning in the mind of the consumer—in other words, repeat business.

In the Exit Mindset, "long-term" and "repeat business" are key operating words—words the buyer of your company wants to hear. These are also the words *you* want to hear while you're developing stability, scalability, profitability, and the goal of more free time. By simply organizing your conversation in a manner conducive to an Exit Mindset, you should be able to achieve those results.

ELEMENTS OF THE CONVERSATION

In business, your company's conversation must reach customers on a variety of levels. You can certainly reach them verbally with the language you use in your marketing copy and advertising. But the exit conversation is meant to involve *all* of the senses: sight, hearing, smell, touch, and taste.

The olfactory sense can be powerful, for example. That's why some real estate agents bake cookies in the kitchen while potential buyers view a house. By filling the rooms with the scent of fresh-baked goods, the agents send a cozy, homey message to the potential buyers, who breathe it in and imagine themselves living there. The same agents may also stage the space with stylish furnishings in order to connect to the buyers' visual sense. Through interior design, they're saying, "This is how your home could look, if you bought this property."

An effective conversation uses these sensory elements, and many others, to guide how the customer thinks and feels. You can do the same in your business. And you must. Even if your company is already successful to the point where you can sell it, you still need to keep the conversation going. You might have the best product and infrastructure around, but if you aren't having a good conversation with your customers and prospects, it will show. Let's look more closely at a few elements of the conversation you may not have thought much about before.

WORK ATTIRE IS CONVERSATION

Yes, what you wear when you're doing business matters. It conveys a nonverbal message about your business. Imagine a customer walking into a hardware store where employees are dressed in pressed suits and ties. There is a degree of incongruence here. When the customer sees that, they start asking themselves questions: *Why are they dressed that way? Are they telling me this is different from a typical hardware store? Are the items going to be more expensive? Are they going to be better?* One thing they know for sure: the experience here will be different from any other hardware store. That is why workers in a hardware store dress in a specific uniform reflecting the type of work they do. Their style of dress communicates to customers that they understand the product because they dress like a person working in the home repairs field.

ENVIRONMENTAL SCENT SPEAKS TO CONSUMER BRAIN

The power of smell goes beyond home-baked cookies. Some offices and hotels harness this power by installing hidden devices that infuse the air with a scent specifically designed to trigger certain feelings that are commonly associated with that smell. The consumer may not consciously register the scent, but they get the message. If you walk into a furniture store and you smell pine, you might start imagining yourself tucked away in a peaceful cabin in the woods. The message from the retailer is that you are in the woods and perhaps this very furniture will help keep that feeling in your home.

Be careful, though. The message on scents cuts both ways. Companies can mess this up if they fail to eliminate unpleasant scents that might turn their customers off; an example can be a musty odor coming from carpeting. In this case, they may be communicating to their consumers a very different message: *We provide you with a service that you want, but we don't care about how you feel about our facilities. You can take it or leave it.* This doesn't make it a good or bad business. Simply, it's a type of unspoken communication that tells a certain story.

YOUR LOCATION SPEAKS TO YOUR CUSTOMERS

You might not think of your physical location as part of the conversation, but it is. Each location says something about the business, creating a perception in the mind of the consumer about the company and its services. Are you in an upscale area? Are you in a rural area? Are you in a single building on a major street, or are you in many scattered smaller locations? What about your digital "locations"? The look and feel of your website speak volumes.

Your location doesn't have to be perfect; it just has to be right for your customers. For instance, Home Depot stores aren't always located right next to other shopping centers. That's okay; they know their customers will go out of their way to shop there.

DAYS AND HOURS OF OPERATION

A store's days and hours of operation are part of the conversation, too. For example, a company by the name of 4-Day Tire Store is only open four days a week. Why would a business limit the days a customer can spend money in their store? It may sound crazy, but the business is sending an intentional message to consumers. Maybe they're communicating "scarcity." Maybe they're communicating, *This isn't a place you drop in when you're on your way to somewhere else—it's a destination you plan for on a specific day.* Or maybe they want consumers to know they'll get a better price there because the store keeps their overhead down. Simply through their name and hours, this business is able to create an entire conversation with the customers that makes the business appear more valuable and interesting to them.

CONVERSATION THROUGH INTERIOR DESIGN

Customers who open the front door of your business immediately start forming ideas about your business based on what they experience when they step inside. The warehouse-like interior of a business like Costco tells the consumer it's a "self-serve" retailer. No one at Costco is going to invite you to sit down while they bring you items to look at. Instead, they display stacks of merchandise piled so high that they need forklifts to move things around. In contrast, a high-end jewelry store will feature a clean, well-lit interior with elegant display cases and a helpful staff. This interior communicates quality and personal attention.

There is no right or wrong message here; you just need consistency between the product positioning and what you want to tell the consumer about your business.

COLORS TALK

Your color palette is part of the conversation, too; it expresses your brand. Your colors might tell customers you are elegant, modern, conservative, or cutting edge. A business I own chose blue, the color of the ocean, as its main color to promote a sense of calm. Blue helps people feel tranquil and open.

Another company uses gold as its main color to convey a sense of wealth and luxury. It all depends on what you're trying to convey. Look around when you visit other offices and stores. Have you ever been in a professional office with red walls? Probably not, but you might have been to a clothing store that has red walls. The point is the choice of colors tells a consumer whether a brand is purposefully designed for them.

MERCHANDISING

With retail companies, merchandising choices also create a dialogue with the consumer. For example, if you move an item from its usual spot to a different shelf, your conversation with the consumer changes. Companies sometimes move products to a different location in a store to interrupt the usual pattern of the conversation. They might even attempt to gamify the process of finding the product the customer is looking for—if shoppers have to look for it in a new section of the store, they might come across other products (which you want them to notice) in their search. Again, it's a form of unspoken conversation with your customers.

PRICING SPEAKS VOLUMES

The pricing model you use is a contributor to the conversation you have with your customers. While some companies have higher prices due to cost issues, others increase their prices because they're adding value to their product, such as quality or service level. Your product pricing speaks volumes to the consumer. You might think of it as merely a number, yet your pricing conveys a significant number of messages that influence the customer's decision whether to buy or ignore your product. This conversation drives, in the consumers' minds, a question, perception, or feeling. Your pricing will attract or repel people without you ever saying a word.

Ideally, you want to sell the maximum number of units of your product to generate maximum revenues based on your pricing model. To accomplish this tricky balance, you must focus on understanding your market and competition. If you don't, two things will happen: (1) you'll lose revenues you could have generated, and (2) you could decrease your valuation.

Your pricing strategy will affect the perception of the buyer of your company. If potential buyers find a discrepancy between the value of the product you are selling and the optimal pricing of that product, they might see that as an opportunity. In this case, they will most likely agree to the company valuation you have assigned, a value they consider to be a bargain. If you're able to use the Exit Mindset to optimize your pricing model, you could achieve a greater valuation that the buyer of your company won't be able to ignore. In the end, this would create higher profits for you, giving you more ability to build better infrastructure and enjoy more free time.

CONVERSATION THROUGH PRODUCT PACKAGING

You may not have ever thought of product packaging as part of the conversation with the consumer, but it, too, communicates a message about your company, whether you realize it or not. Packaging includes physical products in a box, service products, and even digital products. With service products, the "packaging" is the way the service is performed. By performing the same service in different ways, you can create different conversations with the consumer and achieve different results. Therefore, finding the optimal way to deliver the service could determine whether you're having the right conversation with your target consumer or a less-than-optimal conversation.

With physical products, your final packaging impacts your

consumers' perceptions of your product. Will they receive a generic-looking carton with little, if any, branding? Or will they receive a box with a personalized thank you note on it? The delivery method and style can also create a nonverbal dialogue. Whether you deliver through a service or through your own internal delivery system, these choices are all part of your company's nonverbal conversation with customers.

You have many options here. For example, you might start a verbal conversation by sending the customer an email or a text message telling them when the package is on the way. Some companies calibrate such a nonverbal conversation by demonstrating efficiency and competence—they intentionally underpromise and overdeliver on delivery speed and product arrival. You might continue that nonverbal conversation by ensuring that the product arrives in an elegantly designed box and is well packaged.

The nonverbal conversation continues even after the box is opened. The consumer may take comfort from seeing that their electronic device, for example, has been packaged in a way that conforms to the quality of the product. It could have simply been wrapped in bubble wrap, stuffed into a manila envelope, and dropped in a mailbox, but the careful packaging projects a very different message about the relationship between the company and the consumer.

I'm not saying that sending your product in a manila envelope via the postal service sends a bad message in every instance for every company. It might be the perfect way to deliver your product; you're just having a different conversation, one that's aligned with your product and your customer's needs. What I'm saying is that the experience does not necessarily need to convey luxury; if you delivered a standard circuit board by private courier, wrapped in a silk bag, your customer would be confused. The delivery wouldn't be consistent with the company and product. But if you deliver an expensive designer perfume in a basic manila envelope, the customer may find it incongruent with their purchase. There aren't any "good" or "bad" conversations, only the right or wrong ones for the specific business and target consumer.

CONVERSATION VERSUS BRAND

Brand is a partial expression of your conversation with the consumer. It's not the conversation itself. And "brand" can be a confusing concept to people who equate logo and brand. They aren't the same thing; a logo is a component of a brand. Your logo says a great deal about your company and is the identifying image of your brand. The color palette, design, font, and, in video, the motion of a logo combine to leave a particular impression on the consumer, emotionally and intellectually.

Conversation brings together all of the brand and other elements described above and creates perceptions of your company in the consumer's mind. Their experience of your company—through visuals, locations, colors, print ads, verbal communication, and more—helps consumers decide whether they want to do business with you now, later, or never. It's okay if the answer is never; knowing this helps you exclude the people who are not your target consumer, which allows you to get laser-focused on the ones you do want, thereby saving you significant advertising dollars.

The IKEA brand, for example, attracts people who want functional home items at a reasonable cost, by default excluding people who are looking for expensive, fully assembled, high-end furniture. It also attracts customers who understand that the no-frills nature of the store requires them to travel a predetermined path through the showroom. The payment area is almost supermarket-like, where people walk with their carts to a register.

This is vastly different from how other furniture stores operate. The shopper who wants customized furniture and high-level customer service in selecting their furniture isn't going to shop at IKEA. That person knows, by the conversation IKEA has with the public, that this store isn't for them. That's fine. In fact, it's excellent for IKEA, which has used its positioning to become a profitable company. IKEA's conversation is formulated to attract a large number of consumers making less-costly purchases, as opposed to certain other furniture retailers that will (through their verbal and nonverbal conversation) appeal to a smaller segment of customers who perhaps has a larger furniture budget.

People think about your company a certain way because of the conversation you have with them. What they think and how they feel isn't always on a conscious level—it's often subconscious. But it affects whether or not they do business with you.

THE CONSISTENT CONVERSATION

Successful companies spend plenty of time on the conversations I've been discussing so far. You should, too. Here's a simple formula to help you evaluate your company's conversation:

Conversation = nonverbal cues + verbal cues + written communication + verbal communication

As you can see, the conversation has many components; the trick is to align those components. One of the most important jobs of your messaging is to build trust with your customers or clients. That is why your message—across all conversational elements—must be unified and in harmony, with all parts working together. And that's why, once you're engaged in conversation with your customer, you can't contradict yourself.

Conflicting messages undermine your conversation. Imagine if Costco stores had high-end décor rather than a warehouse look. Wouldn't that seem like a contradiction, and a troubling one, if you went there expecting it to look like a no-frills warehouse store? You might not consciously be thinking it, but you'd be aware something is out of sync.

Or, imagine pulling into a Walmart store, but instead of empty parking spots, you encounter a valet in a bow tie. He takes your car for you, then a concierge offers to show you to the right aisle. Do you hear the alarms going off in your head? Immediately you're thinking, *This is nice, but it's not the experience I'm used to, and I'm worried I'm going to pay for it somewhere—probably with higher prices. Maybe I'll just head over to a different no-frills outlet.*

Your message must be consistent. It gets repeated in your company's location, interior design, products, positioning, and prices. It gets repeated in the type of employees you hire. It's even repeated in the lighting your business chooses to use. (There's a reason expensive restaurants don't flood their dining areas with fluorescent lighting—that would create a very different visual conversation than the one they want to have.)

Your conversation must be congruent in every repetition, and congruent with the consumer's expectations. If it's not, the consumer will deem you inconsistent. That doesn't mean you can't introduce something new to your conversation with consumers—the new element just has to be a natural fit with the current conversation, with your target demographics, and with your knowledge of your customer's psychographic profile.

You *can* change the conversation gradually, if, for example, you're shifting your business to a new market. In that case, change the conversation slightly and incrementally, and over time you'll either convert your existing customers to the new conversation or they'll go away, and you'll attract new ones who fit your new business model.

Every conversation requires a delicate balance. You have to study and understand the subliminal, specific messages you are sending so you can predict their effects. This predictability is what leads your customers to acceptance, comfort, and feeling at home with your business, product, or service.

Your product itself doesn't have to offer comfort (meaning a sense of ease in the customer's mind), but the conversation does. If your customer buys a gym membership from you so they can work out every day, they're not necessarily seeking comfort—working out, after all, requires exertion and energy. What they're looking for is a business that gets them, knows them, and delivers a unified message that speaks to the values and services they're seeking.

What does all of this have to do with the Exit Mindset? Well, the more aligned you are with your messaging to the public and your customers, the higher the valuation of your company. Your buyer will see the value in intangibles, such as your consumers' perception of your conversation with them.

Your job is to make sure that your conversation with the consumer is consistent, clear, and organized, and that it has scalable impact that enhances the company's valuation. Thus, every conversation channel must easily mesh with the overall conversation. If you violate that rule, either through thoughtless or willful negligence, the consumer's perception is altered.

Nobody wants to be accused of negligence, but it happens. Thoughtless negligence—failing to notice when things change for the worse—can happen when you don't pay attention and aren't intentional about your conversation with consumers. Willful negligence is knowing you *should* be intentional about maintaining congruency but allowing the conversation to drift, out of laziness or not caring. Either way, the consumer doesn't know why the conversation changed, so the effect is the same.

The consumer *will* notice that something has changed, however. Customers may also subconsciously sense incongruency, even if they can't articulate it. They know when something's out of character. When the ground shifts under consumers like that, it changes how they feel about your company. The question to ask yourself is, *Is what they think and feel about our brand correct, or do we need to change their perception?*

The conversation must remain consistent in interactions between employees and customers, as well. Nobody does this better than Disney. Whether it's a Disney theme park, movie, or merchandise, Disney projects a consistent conversation through every aspect of their interaction with customers. In their theme parks, this is demonstrated by the way the crew dress and behave, the types of eateries they have, the types of rides they offer, and so on. Disney's message is always the same: *We're family friendly.* Customers know Disney World, Disneyland, and any Disney movie are safe places to take their kids. Adults love it, too, as Disney represents some of the best moments in their own childhoods. The whole family is happy. Disney is an expert at providing a continuous, consistent conversation to ensure maximum impact in everything they do or say because they study the conversation inside and out, and keep it congruent, consistent, and maintained in every aspect.

The conversation even impacts how Disney hires. They're extremely diligent with employee backgrounds, dispositions, and demeanors. They're equally meticulous in making sure the people who interact with their patrons continue the safe, magical, family-friendly conversation they've worked hard to create. This is why Disney has exceptional goodwill with its customers and such a robust reputation. Without these distinguishing features, they would just be another amusement park.

Employee–customer interactions are important, no matter what your business is. For instance, consider a high-end hotel versus a mid-range hotel. If you ask an employee of the high-end hotel where the dining area is, they will likely stop what they're doing and walk you to the exact location so you won't have to struggle in finding it. Contrast that with a mid-range place, where employees are more likely to verbally direct you to where it is and continue their work.

Again, it's all about who you're targeting and what messages you want to convey to them, verbally and nonverbally. There is no good or bad. It's all about finding the right fit.

THE CONVERSATION WITH EXISTING CUSTOMERS

Once a business has acquired a customer for one product, and that customer is satisfied, it's significantly easier to introduce them to another product and get repeat business. It's human nature. Most people tend to buy the same car they bought the first time. They're loyal. Some households take this loyalty so seriously, for example, that they may identify themselves as a Toyota family or a Honda family. Therefore, for the car company, acquiring and keeping a customer could mean a long-term and lucrative relationship. Would you like your business to be what an entire family identifies with? That's why you must keep the relevant, intentional, and congruent conversation going.

As mentioned at the beginning of the chapter, "long-term" and "repeat business" are operating words that any buyer of your company will be interested in. They will want to see how you handle your conversation with existing customers, so be prepared to take them step-by-step down the roads you lead your consumers along during their journey toward purchasing your products. The journey can happen in either the physical or the digital manifestations of your business. It's evident in how you welcome a person who enters your business, or how you greet a person who visits your website.

It's recognizable in the color schemes your business is known for, ease of entry, and everything else you do to show the consumer they're "in the right place." You might even provide content the consumer wants to read. The information you make available and how you present it is also part of the conversation. To get it right, you have to understand who you are—who your business is—and be true to how you present yourself to the consumer. Then you have to pay attention to their feedback and make improvements to ensure you're staying congruent with your business model without losing their interest in the conversation.

Showing a buyer you have intentionally designed a congruent conversation that leads to a predictable conclusion—the consumer likes what they're hearing and wants to continue—will give you a better valuation and a higher price for your business. Congratulations! You now have an exit conversation.

CHAPTER 12 EXERCISE

If you are finding it challenging to develop, sustain, or refine your exit conversation, consider these questions:

What conversations does my company engage in with its target market? If not adequate, how can we enhance them?	What message does our physical location convey? If it is not in alignment with our brand, what steps can we take?	Have we utilized all senses to extend our conversation with the customer? If not, what sensory aspects can we incorporate?
What visual and auditory messages are we delivering? If they need improvement, what changes should we make?	How should our employees dress and interact with customers? If changes are needed, what is the plan?	Can customers reach us easily? If not, what steps can we take to improve accessibility?
What do consumers perceive about our company? If perceptions are negative, how will we address them?	How is our brand perceived by consumers? If not positively, what strategies can we adopt to improve?	Is our brand message consistent across all platforms? If not, what steps can we take to ensure uniformity?

EXIT CONVERSATION STRATEGIES

I FIND MOST BUSINESS OWNERS EVENTUALLY understand the value of having a great exit product; and, to a lesser extent, they understand the value of having a great exit infrastructure. Still, many business owners, perhaps most, take conversation for granted. This is short-sighted. The truth is, you can't make a scalable business—one that potential buyers of your company would value—unless you have the right conversation with the consumer. No matter how good your product is and no matter how good your infrastructure is, if you don't have a dialogue that fits the product and infrastructure to the consumer, you're in trouble. The conversation is the piece that allows you to connect with the consumer in a way that makes them value your business.

Potential buyers know that when companies have great

products and great infrastructure, but their conversation with the consumer is lacking, they are at risk for takeovers and purchases that may have lower valuation. Buyers will ask questions. Some will be about the objective measures: How many eyeballs are hitting your website? How many people are coming back to your site? Who's walking into your establishment, and who's buying? Are they coming back? How many are coming back? Other questions will be subjective: How big a fan is the consumer of your product? How much are your consumers really interested in what you have to offer? Are they super into what you have and won't buy anyone else's product, or is their interest just average? How easily could they be swayed to buy someone else's product?

If they identify problems during this question-asking process, the buyer may strategically and intentionally place a lower value on the company, snap it up, and then set about changing the conversation to better fit the consumer. The buyer will then reap the rewards the business owner could have had if they had known what to do.

The outcome of this scenario undoubtedly hurts, but don't think of this approach as malicious—identifying undervalued business opportunities is the prerogative of your prospective buyer. It isn't their fault if you, as the business owner or CEO, failed to maximize the conversation you were having with your customers while you were running the company. It is not their job to fix your problems. Their job is to find the company that represents the best pricing for the value they're getting at the time.

To get the value *you* want from your business, therefore, reframe your thinking about the value of the conversation and brand you have developed. When the brand does its part of the job, and the conversation does its part of the job, then you have both a successful transaction and a successful interaction with customers, who become primed for the next interaction—and you're able to show a potential buyer that they, too, can expect this type of response.

DON'T LET EMOTIONS RULE

Why do so many businesspeople think their valuation is higher than it really is? It happens all the time—either their product, infrastructure, conversation, or a combination thereof is dragging down the entire valuation, but they don't realize it. The reason it's so hard to see this clearly is that our emotions color our perceptions.

If you've ever watched the show *Shark Tank*, you've seen it happen; many contestants overvalue their companies. For example, someone might request ten times the investment their company is worth. Then, it's up to the *Shark Tank* investors to bring their valuation back to earth. You will see this repeated in almost every episode, and it's a situation I want you to avoid. If you take an objective view of your business, you can find and fix many of these things yourself. If you do so, you will raise the valuation of your company, and, should you eventually engage an investor, will more easily obtain leverage during negotiations.

The inventor of the company Ring—the doorbell with a built-in video camera—was on *Shark Tank* a while ago. He had a product, and a certain degree of an infrastructure. Yet he lacked the right conversation needed to generate more sales and attract investors. Most of the sharks on *Shark Tank* did not see the value in the product (proving that not everyone can identify potential), and one of them made an unacceptable offer. The inventor of the product didn't give up. He pressed on with his efforts to scale the company and establish a better product and better infrastructure. But most importantly, he created a very strong, relevant conversation in multiple media, with both the public and investors, to make Ring almost a household word, as well as the generic term for that class of product. The company grew significantly, causing it to garner attention from both the public and investors. In the end, the company was sold to Amazon for a large premium.

I can't promise you the same level of success. However, if you apply the Exit Mindset to your business and succeed in your implementation, then you should be able to achieve higher scale and valuation—which, in the end, means you'll have a successful exit if you decide to undertake one.

Even if you're not selling your business or looking for investors, if your conversation with the consumer isn't where it could be, you're not capitalizing on your entire market potential, and you're not making as much in revenues and profits as you could be. And what that does is create a vicious cycle, so you don't have the money or the freedom to create more time for yourself. A good conversation, as defined here, supported by strong branding, would have created time and added revenues to dedicate to improving your product and your infrastructure.

EXTENDING THE CONVERSATION

A good conversation lasts long beyond the sale of your company. To ensure that takes place, configure the conversation so that it can be transferred easily and seamlessly to the buyer through systemized processes and procedures within the system.

This exit conversation, focused on positioning the company's verbal and nonverbal communication, creates what's called company goodwill. Goodwill is an intangible that has a quantifiable value when it comes to valuation. If your company has goodwill with the public, it possesses a conduit to higher sales, which by extension gives you more revenues to build a better infrastructure that is scalable and can give you more profits and time, all while increasing the value of your business. It's what potential buyers are looking for when conducting valuation on your company and deciding what it's worth.

To assess the value of your conversation with the consumer, take the buyer's point of view. The buyer is looking at the consumer's perception of your products and your business, based first on the branding and then on the conversation you're having with them. Examine that conversation closely, and be honest about what you see. Every interaction tells the consumer something about you.

Digging into this will help you see the conversation as its own business unit, but remember that it's intertwined with your other exit units, product, and infrastructure. For example, the vendors you hire to design your showroom or your website affect the conversation you have with your consumer. If they deliver a carefully thought-out design that reflects what you want to tell your consumer, and it's congruent with your business model, then that will be reflected within the overall conversation. All of the exit systems connect to work together.

HOW TO IMPLEMENT A CONVERSATION STRATEGY

Designing and implementing an exit conversation strategy into your company could be a reasonably easy or a complex project, depending on your situation. Nevertheless, it's crucial for you to get to it if you want to have a successful valuation and increase your profits.

You want to do this right, but there are many ways to go wrong, so let's look at those first. One of the biggest pitfalls that business owners and executives fall into is throwing an entire project—decision-making, planning, deployment, and evaluation—into one bucket. Then, they start drawing from this bucket, depending on the day. It's not unusual for one or two project phases to be implemented while another is neglected. Or you might plan a project and never implement it because you're distracted by a problem or another project. Or you might start implementing a project without taking the time to plan it and identify the metrics by which you'll evaluate whether it's a success. The complexity can be a hindrance. To solve this puzzle, ask yourself these questions:

- How can I break down the exit conversation strategy process into manageable components anybody could complete?
- How do I avoid being overwhelmed?
- How do I deal with the daily distractions that could prevent me from completing the project?
- What's the right project to prioritize? Where do I begin?

Once you've firmed up your exit conversation strategy, it's time to take action.

HOW TO DESIGN AND DEPLOY CONVERSATION CHANNELS

How do you get from where you are now to an exit conversation that has high value to a buyer? You need to thoughtfully consider what channels you want to deploy, and then design your conversation accordingly.

Ideally, you want to design the project cycle of conversation channel deployment in three phases. By breaking the process into phases, you can apply rigor and methods to get from conception to completion with the least amount of chaos and delay. Notice I said *least*; I did not say *no* chaos and delay. People succeed not because everything always runs smoothly, but because they work on it when it doesn't. Chaos, delay, disruption, and unexpected events come with the job, and if you're a business owner or executive in charge of running a division, you must accept that as part of life. Once you accept reality, the job becomes much easier.

The first phase in a conversation channel deployment is exploratory. This is where you make assessments to determine which channel could give you the highest yield and has the best potential for success. Second is the implementation phase of the project, where you're putting the conversation channel together. The third phase is monitoring the results of your work.

PHASE ONE: CHANNEL SELECTION

Start with the list of potential conversation channels you've identified to determine what you would like to work on. Channel examples could include the appearance of your facilities or website, how your product is packaged or sold, how your customer support department handles problems, and the color schemes you use to represent your company. Feel free to add other ideas that pertain to your business. Now cut the list down by two-thirds, so if you started with thirty, you now have ten. Now cut another one-third—if you were at ten, you'll now have six or seven items. From this smaller list, evaluate each channel with the following five factors in mind. This will help you choose the channel you should work on first.

Factor #1: Customer Acquisition Level

For any conversation channel you deploy, whether it's written, verbal, or nonverbal, you should consider what additional customer acquisition level it will generate. How many customers can you expect to acquire with this additional channel? I recommend you choose three figures: high, medium, and low customer acquisition levels. High would be realistic, medium is average, and low is the worst-case scenario. Barring catastrophic results from the lowest figure, you can proceed with the decision to deploy that channel.

Factor #2: Revenue

Next, calculate what added revenue you can expect should the channel be deployed. You won't be able to get a precise figure because you're dealing with an unknown, but apply your knowledge and intuition to make a strategic assessment of the potential results. You know your business and your revenue expectations for new projects. Be realistic in your forecasting. Again, choose a high, medium, and low figure based on realistic, average, and worst-case results. Carefully consider the lowest number. Make sure you can survive the failure if this low number ends up being the actual result of deploying that channel.

To gauge potential failure, consult with your financial specialists for insight into what you can afford to lose. The biggest source of success and failure when undertaking a business project is the assessment of a downside risk. Start directly and simply: If this conversation channel was to fail completely after I spend all this money, time, and resources on it, will my company survive? Will I suffer a major financial disaster?

The eventual outcome of deploying a channel can be challenging to predict, because in planning a conversation channel, you're going to be balancing multiple factors. It's possible that the expected revenues for a planned channel are low while expected customer acquisition numbers for that channel are high. Some businesses prefer a higher customer acquisition number for reasons such as long-term business potential. When you're at this point and trying to decide among several choices weighted between the first two channel selection factors, look to the third one, cost, to narrow your decision.

Factor #3: Budgetary Considerations

If an idea scores high in the first two factors but the cost is beyond your company's financial means, it's not the right channel for your business right now. The reality is, the projected amount of money and resources you need to spend on a conversation channel will have an impact on your overall company budget.

If the deployment is expected to be profitable, but the amount of profit is not impactful, then you must consider eliminating it—unless it produces something for you other than immediate profit, such as high customer acquisition that can be converted into high profits at a later date. The alternative is to choose a different channel that might fulfill your optimal criteria for success.

All of that said, if you sincerely believe your plan will do well for you financially and from a customer acquisition standpoint, you may be able to convince investors to fund the project for you. You will need to present them with a lucrative ROI to make your case.

Factor #4: Implementation Speed

You've chosen your project and you're ready to go, right? Maybe not quite yet; before moving forward, you need to determine how fast you can deploy the channel. If deployment will be quick, it's time to launch. But if the channel would take a long time to implement, you may not want to start with it, even if it meets all the requirements of the first three factors. Defer that channel to a later date, and instead choose a channel you can deploy more quickly, even if it will probably give you a lower yield. You will always be able to come back to the other channels later.

Let me explain: a channel that you've determined will bring you large returns might take you a year to build, and that could be too long to sustain a healthy financial level. You could deplete your existing resources without having another source of income to carry you over in the meantime. Compare that to a conversation channel that might take you a month to implement and deploy but produces half the results. Implementing that channel first would buy you time, maintain your financial health, and get you to the point where you can implement the channel that is the most profitable.

Factor #5: Overall Value

After you have examined your short list of channels, revisit each factor. By now, you'll have a strong sense of which channel is going to give you the most bang for your buck at the lowest degree of risk. Coming up with the final choice is both an art and a science. Look at your quantitative and qualitative data to make a decision.

PHASE TWO: IMPLEMENTATION

In this phase, you'll create a detailed plan for execution. I've broken this complex process down into several key areas.

Vet Your Vendors

Executing your channel deployment plan will most likely require working with external vendors in a variety of verticals and deliverables. You may think of your vendors as part of your infrastructure (they are), but they're also an important part of your conversation. It's not difficult to quantify the impact of a vendor on your revenues when you measure the result. For example, if the conversation channel you're trying to establish is a modified showroom that better represents your company to your consumer, the ROI of that redesign could be measured by the increase in purchases resulting from the redesign. That will tell you how effective the showroom designers were.

Remember, the customer sees everything about your business and processes it subconsciously. You are constantly in dialogue with them during the entire cycle of your interaction with them, whether they tell you or not. So, make sure you're doing your due diligence and hire those vendors who you know can do the best job. The 20 percent extra effort you invest in due diligence might yield 80 percent better results, a faster turnaround, and a better value for your investment with those vendors. The outcome should reflect your business and your brand.

You will also be having a conversation of sorts with the vendors themselves. Because you need to trust them to create the correct conversation channels, you have to establish a vision for the conversation and communicate it clearly to the vendors. Whether you hire someone to design your showroom or your website, they should be skilled in asking the right questions, listening to you, and designing channels that fulfill your vision. Research vendors carefully, choose the best you can afford, and build relationships with them. Treat them right and hold them accountable.

Allocate Cash into Separate Accounts

Be sure to fund each vendor and channel from its own account. There's a reason that big companies allocate individual budgets into separate accounts to fund projects: If every project is drawing funds from the same pot, it can be hard to keep track of separate budgetary limits. If one project goes over budget, even unintentionally, other projects get shortchanged. Projects that run out of money may have to be abandoned, reconsidered, or refunded. Whether you're a large, mid-size, or small company, you should fund every project separately.

You can gain great clarity by segregating the funds for a project, because it forces you to decide exactly how much you're going to invest in it. That makes it easier to figure out your expected return on investment. Then you can track how much you spend versus how much the project delivers. Separating accounts also prevents you from dipping into funds critical to your business. Employee payroll, for example, should be in its own account. Companies that don't do this run the risk of coming up short. You never want paychecks to bounce.

Open as many accounts as you need. Open ten. Open a hundred. If you're worried about fees, compare a few dollars a month with the cost of overfunding a project that may not have been as important as it first seemed, or underfunding a project that could have transformed your business. Compare those few dollars with the cost of not paying your people because money meant for salaries was spent on something else. Separate your projects and segregate the funds. You will see your projects from a whole new perspective.

Assign Team Members and Accountability Metrics

When you develop conversation channels, you have to put the right people in charge and identify metrics for their accountability. Even if the conversation channel is nonverbal, you need a way to measure its performance and someone to take responsibility for ensuring performance goals are met.

Say you hire a chief designer for a new store you want to open. You want to sell reasonably priced clothing and you're allocating $5 million to have the place designed and built. You talk to the building designer about the conversation the design is going to communicate to the consumer. The designer has to create the perception for the target consumer that they're in the right store—the store that knows them and understands their needs. That store has to communicate through its design the lower price for this clothing.

Communicating all of this to the designer is a necessary first step, but far from your last. As the design unfolds, how will you know if it's hitting the right notes? Just walking into the store and saying, "I think this is it," isn't enough. You need metrics.

You might have to sit down with the designer and a focus group that represents your target shopper to define those metrics. Once the metrics are set, the designer—and only the designer—is responsible for meeting them. They may have a whole team of people working on the building and you may have another team working on the project as part of an infrastructure expansion, but ultimately *one person* has to be accountable to making sure the conversation communicates your intent. Assigning that responsibility to a team doesn't work. Each person will have a different interpretation of what you want; if it succeeds, everyone will take credit, but if it fails, no one will take the blame.

Too often, I've seen business owners at small companies, with thirty or fewer employees, hesitate to make any one person accountable for the success of an important project. In these businesses, there is a tendency to spread the responsibility around and to tolerate poor performance. Don't do that. Whatever the size of your business, establish clear metrics and assign someone to meet them. Either the person meets them, or they don't. Either way, hold them accountable.

The flip side is that by making a person accountable, you're giving them visibility when they succeed. Often, the people who are most reliable are not the same people who talk about their accomplishments. Taking on this responsibility gives them an opportunity to be seen in a different light, and to receive the due credit for a job done right. Ultimately, *someone* has to own the success of this channel, whether it's someone you assign or yourself.

Establish an Acceptable Performance and Completion Date

It's easy to fall into the trap of assuming people know what you want and expect and when you need it delivered. But if you don't tell them, they can't know. To get good work done in a timely manner, you have to clearly communicate your expectations and quantify the end results. Don't allow people to use the quantity of work they're doing as a measure of progress. People tell you they're working on this or that, which gives the illusion things are moving, but in most cases, people are very tactical and will lose track of the larger goal. You may only discover that you're falling behind deadlines when it's too late. So you must ask about the deadline and if it's going to be met. And if it isn't, then there better be a good reason.

When someone on my team or a supplier owes me a project, a product, or a service, I verify three things: What is the deliverable? What is the expectation? What is the deadline? Both of us need to be on the same page with what I am getting and when I am getting it, and I need to know what they believe about the deliverable and the deadline. Will it be what I expect, and do they believe they will get it to me on time? Is there a possibility it will be early or late? That's all crucial information.

One tactic for managing performance is to set clear expectations by using milestones. Establish regular check-ins to see how the project is progressing—those check-ins constitute a deadline accountability system. Make the milestones visible to everyone involved. This eliminates any confusion about when tasks and deliverables are due. You should set up a reasonable agreement both sides are happy with, and that you're satisfied with, in terms of their delivering on time in the quality you're looking for.

PHASE THREE: MEASURE CONVERSATION CHANNELS

It's common, during the daily business grind, to lose track of the key performance indicators (KPIs) of a conversation channel. If that happens, you'll face several questions for which you don't have the answer. Should the channel be maintained or continued? Should more resources be poured into it? Or should it be completely eliminated because of nonperformance?

You will never know the answers to these questions unless

you have data, whether subjective or objective. That's why it's important to assign accountable KPI team leaders to regularly update you on the performance of those initiatives.

Assign Team Leaders

In the third phase of designing and deploying an exit conversation, assign team leaders to monitor KPIs and other results from particular channels once they have been established. Which indicators you choose to monitor in your conversation channels depend on the channels themselves. If you have an existing channel and you're making changes to it, the accountability leader should measure the KPIs before and after the transformation. If you have a brick-and-mortar retail business and you redesign your showroom, for example, you might track how many people walk into the showroom and how long they stay, and analyze their foot-traffic pattern. You could look at the percentage of those people who actually make a purchase, the number of items purchased, the average cost of each item, and the total amount they spend. You can also track repeat customers and their purchasing habits. It's the team leader's job to make sure these kinds of numbers are tracked and reported to you at least monthly.

From those reports, you'll be able to see at a glance whether the conversation channel transformation affected consumers' interactions with your business. You'll see if the response was positive or negative, and in what respect it was positive or negative. If the report is showing positive results month after month and suddenly there's a dip in one or more of the KPIs, you'll know that you need to look into it. For example, maybe you see a reduction in the size of the average purchase. As part of your assessment, you take a look at your showroom and realize all the higher-priced items are in the back, so most consumers end up not seeing them. Or because all the couches in a furniture store are grouped together, instead of sitting with matching tables and related furniture, you're losing sales opportunities.

These are examples of actions you could take in response to the data you review. Perhaps you would design aisles in a way that influences traffic flow to expose customers to the important items they should be purchasing, thus promoting a higher transaction per customer. Or perhaps you group products together in ways that suggest to the customer how they could be used at home.

If you're not getting reports that show deviations in your KPI, you won't have the opportunity to adjust.

Be Ready to Eject

Once you have the channels set up and running and you're getting regular reports, decide whether the results prove worthy of the expenditures you're incurring to support them every month. Sometimes it doesn't make sense to stick with a conversation channel.

The decision to stick with a channel or end it can be difficult, but you must be realistic. Don't continue to put resources into a conversation channel that just isn't working. If there's a deviation in the results, figure out whether the cause of the shift is within your control. If it isn't, and if you're spending money and not getting the results you need, then cut your losses. Any good business person must possess this skill—the willingness—to stop throwing good money after bad, no matter how large the initial investment. Ending a project you've sunk a lot of resources into doesn't mean you're indecisive. It's a sign of a person who's able to make strategic calculations around the odds and risks of winning and losing, how much one can stand to win or lose, and the potential for catastrophic failure. Once you adopt that skill and line of thinking, you'll find it extremely easy to make decisions with no regrets.

Knowing whether to pull the plug is an art and a science. If business was pure science, computers could run your company for you. Computers are great in any number of situations, but as of yet they can't anticipate conversations and make judgments about them like you can. But who knows? With the rapid development of artificial intelligence, maybe they will learn to do that too.

But be absolutely certain a channel isn't yielding the results you want before ending it. The results from a new conversation channel can take time to realize, and I've seen excellent results from channels emerge later than expected.

How many times have you stopped working toward a goal only to realize later you had almost achieved it? Think about looking for a city street, and just as you're about to give up, you see it straight ahead. People often stop short of success, not knowing how close they are. Knowing whether to quit or keep going is a combination of instincts, belief, and understanding the path you're on. There's no hard-and-fast rule you can follow in making this decision. You just have to use your KPIs and instincts together, side by side. If running a company were easy, everyone would do it.

Resist the Gambler Mentality

It's hard to pull the plug on a project you believe in and are invested in. It's almost personal. But allowing what I call the "gambler mentality" to take over could be catastrophic. It goes like this: "I've put so much into this; it's got to pay off soon!"

Focusing on sunk costs can put you on the path toward significant losses—even total loss. Always calculate your budgets and the probabilities of business continuity when you design and implement your conversation channels. Figure out how you can spread your financial resources to maximize the result that will keep your business going for the long term. You should never undertake a project you don't have the budget and resources to finish, and you should know where you stand on this *before* you start, not after you've invested resources. Starting a conversation channel without making this calculation practically guarantees its failure and definitely guarantees a big waste of money.

You may start a channel with the expectation it will give you a certain result, and that's fine if you also know exactly what milestone results are needed for you to control the outcome. How much does the channel need to generate, and when? What do the early trends have to look like for the project to get there by that time, and what is needed for it to be on track? If it does not meet the milestones on time, can you stop it without taking the whole company down? I've personally had major successes working this way, but it requires planning and discipline. You can't let your emotions get in the way, and you have to rely on your best decision-making skills to make the final call, including what you knew when you started the channel and what you have learned since.

The caveat to all these decisions is that sometimes you do have to take that big risk and put it all on the line. The only time to risk major failure is when the company's on the edge of failure anyway and it seems that nothing can save it. When you're faced with ultimate and complete failure, you have to be agile and make decisions for the business that you would never make if the business were thriving. Desperate times indeed call for desperate measures.

TAKE STEPS NOW

Start now. Shift your perspective from business owner to business buyer and see the true value of your business based on product, infrastructure, and conversation. Have you given your product market viability, future sustainability, and growth potential? Your company might have a great infrastructure and the right conversation with the consumer, but if you don't have the right product, then all other efforts are in vain.

Have you designed and built the right infrastructure for production and scalability? Bad infrastructure is one of the main reasons for undervaluation of a company. Smart buyers take advantage of this fact, knowing they can fix the problems and resell your business for a much higher valuation. Don't let this happen to you. Be proactive and get your infrastructure in order.

Are you having a consistent, authentic conversation with your customers? Your conversation goes beyond the spoken or written word to encompass every interaction, every impression, and all communications with the consumer. Even the best product, manufactured within the best infrastructure, cannot sell itself. Your conversation connects your business to the consumer, and how well you're able to execute that conversation impacts profits and valuation.

CHAPTER 13 *EXERCISE*

Consider these questions to guide your development of an effective exit conversation, maximizing your company's value and appeal to potential buyers:

Who is drawn to your business and buying your product? If not ideal, what is your strategy to attract the right audience?

1

Are customers making repeat purchases? If not, how will you encourage them?

2

What is the proportion of returning customers? If low, how will you increase it?

3

What are your website metrics? If suboptimal, what changes will you make?

4

Are your consumers loyal fans of your products? If not, what will you do to build loyalty?

5

How many customers do you foresee with an additional channel (high, medium, low)? If not enough, how will you boost it?

6

What revenue target and timeline does a new channel need for success? If inadequate, what are your improvement plans?

7

PART FIVE

FINALLY! MAKING THE SALE

CHAPTER 14

PLANNING YOUR EXIT

ONCE YOU'VE GAINED AN EXIT MINDSET, YOU will know when it's time to sell your company. But what if you don't have a specific event or revenue or profit figure in mind as a selling point? Even creating a basic exit plan is a smart move, because it's important to express your wishes for the future of your business. It's not something you want to leave to chance.

Of course, how you plan to sell the company has a great impact on what you need to accomplish in advance of the closing date. In the coming sections, I will cover some of the ways you can transfer the ownership of the company. But, for now, let's assume your plan is to simply sell the company to someone, some company, or some entity. What needs to be done as far out as twenty-four months from the sale? What happens in the next year, as you count down to twelve months from the sale, the moment when you should actually be putting the company up for sale publicly and negotiating offers? And after that, what happens in the months following the listing of the company?

As you can see, selling your business takes time. A broker I know was working with a known mid-size company on its plan to sell. The owner had been in the business since his father had started the company many years ago and, frankly, he wanted to do other things with his time. So the broker sat down with the owner to determine how much he wanted to sell the company for. The figure they agreed on was $5 million, leaving roughly $3.7 million after taxes. Once all the numbers were confirmed, the plan was put into action, but much remained to be done.

As the broker tells the story, he had been doing the once-a-year analysis with this client for three years, and this was the first year that there appeared to be a good chance the company would be reaching the $5 million revenue mark, a figure which they felt would translate into a sales price of the same amount. So, results aren't instant, but when you have focused on a target, the path is straightforward. The company sold two months short of the twenty-four-month period and for a quarter-million over the $5 million base they had set. A happy ending for all!

One last caveat: There are special situations that could throw your plan out the window. They might come in the form of a problem or an opportunity that comes your way, so keep your eyes open. If you have an opportunity to develop a specific market, or product, or technology, for instance, then your company could sell for a hefty premium. The window of opportunity may be brief—once you've attracted competitors, that premium could be reduced and you're back to using your original numbers. So keep your eyes open and keep growing and innovating. Bottom line: If you're selling, then sell at the right time.

SELLING FOR OPTIMAL RETURNS

There are as many ways to sell a company as you can imagine. Familiar methods include a simple sale with the buyer paying in full, a sale with seller financing, or a sale with a portion of the selling price paid at closing (for example, 80 percent) and the balance paid in performance payments after a specific number of years. Then there are more unusual ways to transfer ownership, such as turning the company into an employee-sponsored benefit plan (ESOP), turning it over to your children in exchange for a percentage of the revenues for life, selling off the retail portion and keeping the manufacturing, or the reverse, keeping the retail and selling off the manufacturing. You can sell the company for stock in a larger company instead of cash. You can decide to keep the buildings if they're valuable, and then sell the company and rent the buildings to the new owner. And you can also decide to give the business to your children, or sell it to them over a period of years, generating a fixed monthly income that can be used to fund retirement. Options abound. So the questions become, What is your goal in transferring ownership of the company? And what is the best way to optimize your income from the sale, if that is your goal, or optimize the result you want if money isn't the goal?

If your goal is to give the company to your children and then receive a lifetime monthly income from it, that is very doable and, frankly, pretty simple. Get your accountant and attorney together and skip the selling process; make the arrangements and do the transfer. The monthly payment should be close to what it might have been after taxes and based on a conservative rate of return. By structuring the deal with the seller (you) still holding property deeds and related assets, you get the protection of having a decent-size fund within the company for these payments.

If the goal is to sell the company for the highest after-tax figure, then it's important to view every offer in light of the tax implications. Depending on how a deal is structured, the net after tax can be wildly different. For example, doing the deal one way could result in, say, $10 million net cash, and doing it another way could result in $8 million net cash. So, it's critical your accountant is deeply involved in the offers and is helping you determine how they play out to your benefit. That said, everything you do—other than getting a wire for the entire amount in your account on closing day—increases your risk in the deal. That risk has to be compensated.

Do you go along with some performance-based formula paying you, for example, 85 percent now and as much as another 30 percent over two or three years? If it's the only offer, then you may have no choice, but you are likely better off taking a cash offer for less than the overall total—maybe 92–93 percent of the deal amount—rather than 85 percent now and maybe not ever seeing the rest. What looks bulletproof isn't actually risk free. Many things can cause damage to your settlement, so perhaps carrying the sale for two to three years is unnecessary unless the risk portion is small and the potential reward portion is worth the risk.

A better way to handle the idea of increasing revenues when the new owner takes over is to take a small percentage of the gross revenues, either completely or over a certain figure. As the seller, you might take a slightly lower percentage at closing so you can participate in those increases over time. For example, say your company has done a number of promotions over the last year that you believe will increase gross revenues for the next two years for the new owner. They have been expensive, and you would like to get something for this investment. Monthly average revenues for the last year have been $400,000, so you add to the deal a clause that the new owner will report gross revenues to you for the next twenty-four months. In any month when the gross exceeds $400,000, they agree to pay you 10 percent of the amount over $400,000. This way, you gain as the new ownership gains, and it's easy to track on a monthly basis.

So, involve your professionals, be firm but flexible, and realize there are dozens of ways to make a deal work, so be open to all of them.

PLANNING AND ADVERTISING THE SALE

All the years of hard work and sweat and stress have come down to this: It's time for you to cash out, retire, or maybe take a rest and open another business six months or a year from now. You are ready to put your company up for sale.

Later in this chapter, I will lay out a rough timeline for what happens each month once you make this decision and implement it. It's a twelve-month timeline, but maybe yours turns out to be only half that long because a quick, profitable sale falls into your lap. In the schedule I've laid out, I've allowed for a sale that doesn't happen that quickly. Whatever the timeline, you should work efficiently toward your goal. Every day you are inattentive to the daily work of running your company is likely two days longer your sale is delayed. You have to stay and run the company.

When you are ready to move forward, you want to, in order:

1. Confirm everything you plan to do with your life partner/ spouse, your children, and anyone else important in your life.
2. Make the decision to tell the staff now or wait until later.

Arrange this very delicate meeting so there are no interruptions, answer all questions honestly, and advise your staff what the plan is for them.

3. Arrange separate meetings with your professionals. Again, you aren't interested in being talked out of your decision, but putting them on notice that you are going to need cooperation, documents, history, and direction. Each one, CPA, attorney, insurance person, etc., has a role to play to assist you in closing a fair and equitable deal.

4. Plot out a schedule (use the one in the "Month-by-Month Sale Plan" section below) of what you expect to happen and when to keep you on track, to remind you of who you need to contact, and to make sure the process is flowing.

Your next decision is to determine how you will sell the business. You can accomplish this in a few ways, from selling it yourself to hiring a major national bank or investment firm to represent you. Unless you have a huge company, the latter would not be a viable option for you. Typically, you will choose to engage a broker of some kind to represent your company. Selling it yourself is not only time consuming and full of potholes and pitfalls, but it dissolves the distance you need in order to make solid, objective decisions as the need arises. Hiring a broker costs money, but finding a reputable one, preferably specializing in your industry, will more than pay you back for your investment. They have been through this before and know what is next, what is later, and what to expect at every step.

Your choices generally are local business brokers, national business brokers, or industry-specific business brokers. This decision will be based on the type of business you're selling. If it's a local business, then a local broker is appropriate. If it sells nationally or has national reach, use a national business broker. If you are in a less well known and understood industry, or believe your potential buyer is within your industry, then an industry-specific broker is for you.

Consult with others who have sold their companies in the last two years, and pick up referrals from your professionals and other respected businesspeople. You're sure to come up with a few brokers that match the criteria described above. Start with them. Add people to your list until you have four or five brokers, at least, bidding to represent your interests. Meet with them, make notes as to services and costs, and rank them based on what you believe they will do for you and the sale. My advice to you is not to sign on for more than six months. If the broker is doing a good job, you can extend it another six months.

Each one in the first interview should request some numbers or your financials in order to give you a range for their idea of the asking price. Give them the materials once you have each signed a nondisclosure agreement (NDA), which your attorney will supply. From your interviews, have them bring you a proposal for what they will do for you, in writing, including their fees, as well as referrals and a list (without names) of the sales they have concluded in the last twelve months.

In the meantime, you will have met with your accountants and will have some idea of your company's valuation. You could also use the information in preceding chapters to come up with your own valuation range and use it for comparison to the brokers' valuation ranges. All this information should help you make a decision as to which broker to hire.

NOTES TO KEEP IN MIND

Throughout this book, I've described many different benefits of selling your company with a sound exit strategy. There are, foremost, financial benefits. You've worked hard to build a business—why let it sell for anything less than what it's truly worth? Equally important are the quality-of-life benefits. After all the work and the long days and nights, a sound exit strategy can bring you the ways and means to take on new experiences, with time and money to support that goal. And let's include the benefits to your legacy—ensuring the financial well-being of your family and others with the rewards you earn from selling your company. You can enjoy all of these benefits, and others, but allow me to give you some added advice as you move toward selling:

- Don't sell your company yourself. There are roughly 1,000 reasons to listen to the old adage: "An attorney who represents himself has a fool for a client." The same applies to acting as your own broker.
- You can make a broker an offer to cut the commission on the base in exchange for an increase/bonus if the business sells for 10 percent or 20 percent over your internal base price. That's a great way to boost incentive for a quick and worthwhile sale.
- Always provide the broker with a list of companies to approach first and give those companies two weeks to respond and express interest; then move on to regular general public promotions.
- Always provide your broker with a "Do Not Speak To" list. These will be people and entities to whom no information at all is given, regardless of whether they've agreed to sign a nondisclosure agreement. Your broker should understand not to forward an NDA to these parties.
- For those parties with a legitimate interest in buying your company, always share information under an NDA, all the

time, every time. Any violation of this—including your own violation—may be grounds for immediate termination of any agreement.

- Be reasonable, and don't wait too long to agree to a final sale. Usually, the first deal that meets your reasonable requirements is good enough to pursue and close. Trying to get the perfect deal might extend your sales window beyond what's useful. Be realistic.

MONTH-BY-MONTH SALE PLAN

If you don't have your own plan for getting to the point of a sale, you can refer to this shorthand version of what you could be doing each month. It assumes optimal situations; your situation may be drastically different. It's important to modify this template monthly as variables develop or as you take certain actions. Understand that not everything happens in a straight line, but it all happens at some point. This is a general outline meant to give you guidance, but is in no way intended to replace legal counsel.

- **Thirteenth Month:** Meet with an attorney, CPA, and brokers. Get valuation ranges and create your own if a CPA cannot. Select the broker, and work with them on a promotional plan and a "who to approach" list.
- **Twelfth Month:** Gather paperwork necessary for historical information. Use the "who to approach" list first for two weeks. Then start advertising the sale.
- **Eleventh Month:** Increase advertising to a broader set of potential buyers. Look for patterns among those inquiring and declining, especially those who discover no components of your company that need fixing.

- **Tenth Month:** By now, and depending on your company, you may have one or two initial offers. Always take all offers seriously unless the offering price is so far below your valuation that it's unworkable. Compare offers, and if none make the grade, negotiate as you can—but don't expect to get $30 million from a $5 million offer.
- **Ninth Month:** If you haven't yet, you may be now receiving serious offers that include requests for information that signal the beginning of informal due diligence. You should be ready to sign a formal offer, pending due diligence. Likely, there's been some negotiation and back and forth and, other than issues that arise during the due diligence phase, there's a deal on the table. Set the closing for ninety days from signing to keep the ball rolling and moving toward the closing. Make sure you have appropriate legal counsel for these proceedings.
- **Eighth Month:** Due diligence continues with issues and questions.
- **Seventh Month:** Resolving all due diligence issues, rework the deal based on changes.
- **Sixth Month:** If your deal started in the tenth or ninth month, then you are ready to close. You're ahead of the schedule. If you haven't started a deal, this is the month you really need to find a buyer and settle a deal to stay on schedule. If your broker agrees and it looks promising, arrange a closed bidding situation among three or more interested parties. However, if this isn't an option, continue with advertising the sale.
- **Fifth Month:** If you have expected that at this point you would be making your exit, then you have to have a deal resolved this month and due diligence started. If you don't have a deal done here, it's long past time to figure out what

is wrong. Pricing? Presentation? Lack of interested buyers? The economy? Find a solution and fix it fast.

- **Fourth Month:** Resolve outstanding due diligence and any issues or questions.
- **Third Month:** Prepare for closing by the end of the month. You are still sixty days ahead of the end of twelve months.

COMPLETING THE SALE

As with the abbreviated calendar above, what follows is a brief, broad-brush approach to explaining what happens in a sale. Every sale is different, yet there are common elements.

Every sale has a closing date. This is the date by which everything committed to for the closing must be done. The buyer wires the funds or deposits a check into an escrow account. The seller ensures that all bills created by the company to this point have been paid in full, including payroll, if the pay period extends into the new owner's time. Documents that have been analyzed by both attorneys and CPAs are now available for signature.

If there are accounts receivable and inventory, or both, then the seller brings accountings for both and squares up with the buyer, based on previously agreed-to levels. For example, perhaps the contract calls for $100,000 in accounts receivable being turned over to the buyer and $100,000 of inventory at cost being turned over as well. The seller provides documents of $103,000 of accounts receivable and $104,000 of inventory. Thus, the buyer owes the seller an additional $7,000 at the closing. Usually, these numbers are done the day before and the seller avoids doing business on the last day. The opposite situation can also occur, in which the numbers are lower than contracted and the seller owes a check to the buyer for that amount.

If real estate is involved, the closing will include a real estate closing. All the keys, codes, combinations, passwords, and safe information are transferred. It's already assumed the buyer has opened their own bank accounts and is ready to do business after the closing takes place. Dozens of documents are generally signed and witnessed. In many cases, there is a call for celebration, which usually takes place with the close principals first and possibly later with the staff.

Most of the time, the seller will have already agreed to stay on for thirty or sixty days to answer questions, so the closing is often not the last time buyer and seller meet. But, sometimes it is and the company is metaphorically moved to the buyer's location.

Congratulations! A successful sale of your business has taken place. It is easy to get wrapped up in the mechanics of the sale and forget the underpinning that caused the sale to occur, which are the product, the infrastructure, and the conversation. Without these three foundations in place, the sale could be a lot more complicated and not necessarily yield the success you are looking for. The intent of this chapter was to fast forward to the end, but remember, the end is made possible through the beginning, and the beginning is a means to the end. The exit mindset is always the beginning.

CONCLUSION

MY MISSION IN THIS BOOK WAS TO GIVE YOU THE tools to adopt an Exit Mindset so you can build a business that generates even more profits for you and increases your company's valuation—whether you end up selling it or not. I want you to develop an exit product, an exit infrastructure, and an exit conversation so you will be able to pay your people well. And as your business grows, I want you to be able to hire more people, make contributions to your community, and benefit the economy. That's the outcome I'm hoping for and that you can achieve!

My secondary goal makes the first mission possible: I hope to help you see your business from a buyer's perspective. To see its true valuation objectively. Make your company's value your North Star. Strive toward adding to that value, and never lose sight of that goal. The alternative is working for maybe decades, only to discover that your business is worth much less than the years of life you've invested in it. You could come away with little to show for your efforts and may not even be able to sell the company.

I want you to create an exit business so that when the time comes to sell, you'll get a price you deserve. Of course, you may not want to sell your exit business at all. A company that allows you to make greater income and have more time may be a company you want to keep. After all, you may not find a better rate of return on any other investment out there!

Once you shift to an Exit Mindset, find a way to maintain it. Sliding back into the same old rut—the daily grind—doesn't have to be inevitable. That kind of thinking will drag you down and take your business down too. Too often, people sabotage their own success. They do whatever's the most complicated or complex, thinking the harder it is, the greater the outcome. Instead of getting caught up in the never-ending barrage of information, focus on your product, infrastructure, and conversation. Get laser focused and you'll find clarity with this new, cleaner, simpler lens.

I want you to know that I take this mission personally, and will continue to help through my website, ExitMindset.com, where you will find additional valuable resources, worksheets, and regular updates on Exit Mindset principles that will keep you on track.

I applaud you for completing this journey through the Exit Mindset, and wish you all the success you deserve!

ABOUT THE AUTHOR

REM OCULEE, an accomplished entrepreneur, CEO, and investor, has spent over two decades establishing successful companies. His wide-ranging experience, shaped by both successes and setbacks, has honed his approach to strategy and execution. His strategic framework, built on product focus, scalable infrastructure, and innovative consumer conversation channels, has contributed to massive growth in numerous businesses.

Rem's approach to exits, valuation, and acquisitions focuses on the entire lifecycle of a company to maximize value. His ability to leverage collaborations, along with his focus on the strategic components of exit transactions, has helped many businesses increase their market valuation, navigate acquisitions, and achieve significant revenue growth.

In addition to contributing his time to help the business community, Rem is a martial artist, holding a black belt in Shotokan Karate and actively practicing mixed martial arts. Balancing his professional pursuits, Rem dedicates his leisure time to family, sports, and philanthropy, reflecting the success he espouses in *Exit Mindset.*